D0354608

EXPERIENCE

# SHANGHAI

# ⊙ Walking Eye App

Your Insight Guide now includes a free app and eBook, dedicated to your chosen destination, all included for the same great price as before. They are available to download from the free Walking Eye container app in the App Store and Google Play. Simply download the Walking Eye container app to access the eBook and app dedicated to your purchased book. The app features an up-to-date A to Z of travel tips, information on events, activities and destination highlights, as well as hotel, restaurant and bar listings. See below for more information and how to download.

## MULTIPLE DESTINATIONS AVAILABLE

Now that you've bought this book you can download the accompanying destination app and eBook for free. Inside the Walking Eye container app, you'll also find a whole range of other Insight Guides destination apps and eBooks, all available for purchase.

## DEDICATED SEARCH OPTIONS

Use the different sections to browse the places of interest by category or region, or simply use the 'Around me' function to find places of interest nearby. You can then save your selected restaurants, bars and activities to your Favourites or share them with friends using email, Twitter and Facebook.

## FREQUENTLY UPDATED LISTINGS

Restaurants, bars and hotels change all the time. To ensure you get the most out of your guide, the app features all of our favourites, as well as the latest openings, and is updated regularly. Simply update your app when you receive a notification to access the most current listings available.

## TRAVEL TIPS & DESTINATION OVERVIEWS

The app also includes a complete A to Z of handy travel tips on everything from visa regulations to local etiquette. Plus, you'll find destination overviews on shopping, sport, the arts, local events, health, activities and more.

## HOW TO DOWNLOAD THE WALKING EYE

Available on purchase of this guide only.
1. Visit our website: www.insightguides.com/walkingeye
2. Download the Walking Eye container app to your smartphone (this will give you access to both the destination app and the eBook)
3. Select the scanning module in the Walking Eye container app
4. Scan the QR code on this page – you will be asked to enter a verification word from the book as proof of purchase
5. Download your free destination app* and eBook for travel information on the go

* Other destination apps and eBooks are available for purchase separately or are free with the purchase of the Insight Guide book

# CONTENTS

# SHANGHAI
# OVERVIEW

**Time is turning full circle in Shanghai. Back in the roaring 1920s and '30s, the 'Pearl of the Orient' was one of the globe's most fashionable and talked-about cities. An economic boom fuelled creativity and the thriving nightlife scene became world famous. Fast-forward 90 years, and much the same is happening again.**

China's most progressive, western-facing city has benefitted big time from globalisation. Pudong, on the east bank, little more than wasteland until the early 1990s, now looks like the set of a sci-fi film. Neon-glowing elevated highways seem to fly through the air, and the rocket-like Oriental Pearl Tower pierces the sky against the canyon of glittering skyscrapers framing Lujiazui district in Pudong. But west of the river, glorious old Shanghai can still be found in the stunning neoclassical and Art Deco buildings along the Bund, and in the architecture left behind in the old Concessions and the Chinese *longtang* (lane) neighbourhoods.

In this spirited city of 23 million people, tea stores, dim sum kiosks and Buddhist temples sit alongside contemporary art galleries, franchised coffee shops and BMW showrooms. The Shanghainese are savvy shoppers, and the city centre is saturated with glitzy malls and brand boutiques, while at the same time, you can also find traditional offerings. After working or shopping, city dwellers like to kick back with a foot or body massage in one of the numerous spas and massage parlours citywide.

Shanghai's nightlife and dining scene can now challenge Hong Kong and Singapore. The best ways to enjoy the city's after-dark splendour include strolling along the riverside Bund or sipping a cocktail in one of several sky-high cocktail lounges.

Street signs are in English and Chinese, and English is increasingly understood in the main neighbourhoods (though not by taxi drivers!). The extensive and continually expanding metro system is modern, efficient and cheap, and Shanghai is a very safe city day and night – so go explore.

# IN THE MOOD FOR...

## ... STREET LIFE

Shanghai life is lived on the streets. Vibrant French Concession boulevards like **Huaihai Road** (see page 95) and **Yongkang Road** (see page 106) blend heritage architecture with boutiques and cafes, and day-night street theatre. From French finery to imposing British-built mansions, the streets around the Bund are filled with history in various states of upkeep. Take in the renovated architecture at **The Bund** (see page 28) and **Rockbund** (see page 32), but don't miss the grungier yet wonderfully lively back streets, including **Sichuan** and **Fuzhou** roads (see page 42).

## ... 1930S GLAMOUR

Nowhere evokes the glamour of 1930s Shanghai more than the iconic **Peace Hotel** (see page 30) whose splendid Art Deco interiors have been revamped and reopened. A drink at **Yongfoo Elite** (see page 91), a fabulous Concession-era villa chockfull of period antiques, will transport you back in time, as will a night of jazz music at the **House of Blues and Jazz** (see page 37). Revive the glamorous 'Paris of the Orient' look with a figure-hugging *qipao* dress by **local designer Lu Kun** (see page 63).

## ... FINE DINING

Whereas fine dining was once restricted to deluxe hotels, high-quality Chinese and international cuisines are now offered across a city with an avowed ambition to be recognised globally as a dining destination. Nowhere sates modern Shanghai's penchant for see-and-be-seen dining and riverside views better than **M on the Bund** – the expansive terrace is a superb destination for Bund brunching. Across the road, celebrity chef Jean Georges Vongerichten has three supremely popular restaurants at **Three on the Bund**, while inventive European cuisine is on the menu at French chef Paul Pairet's **Mr & Mrs Bund** (see page 34 for all above). Pairet is also the gourmand genius behind Shanghai's most in-demand table, **Ultraviolet** (see page 143) which serves a choreographed 20-course 'molecular' menu to just 10 diners a night. Book months in advance for this hotspot. Shanghai's homegrown celebrity chef Tony Lu has a growing empire of award-winning restaurants. Among these, **Fu 1088**, (see page 157) serves classic Shanghainese dishes in a lavishly decorated heritage villa, while **Fu He Hui** (see page 157) is a stylish Zen-inspired restaurant serving creative Chinese vegetarian prix fixe menus.

## ... RETAIL THERAPY

Retail revenues are emerging as a key driver of the local economy, and shopping is an acknowledged obsession with the newly affluent classes. Today's consumers are increasingly spoilt for choice. Premium purchasing is offered in the glossy malls that stretch along **Huaihai Road** and **Nanjing Road West** (see page 80), while the narrow lanes of **Xintiandi** (see page 52) attract a boutique brand clientele to shop, lunch and ostentatiously sip coffees on outdoor terraces. Young Shanghai fashion designers show-case their latest couture, jewellery and accessory lines in restored houses on **Fumin Road** and **Changle Road** (see page 94), on the corner of Fuzhou Road and **The Bund** (see page 36), and at the **Xintiandi Style** mall, a dedicated hub for Chinese design talent (see page 52). The **Shanghai IFC** mall (see page 118) in Pudong is a smart destination for label-led shoppers.

Specialist shops and markets abound. Lustrous gem-quality pearls can be found at **Hongqiao Pearl City** (see page 153); **Tianshan Tea City** (see page 151) is a three-storey emporium of fine tea; a dazzling array of silks, cashmeres and linens are on display at the **South Bund Fabric Market** (see page 58); the Cang Bao Lou **Antiques 'Ghost Market'** (see page 57) is a chaotic mixture of genuine antiques and pure kitsch. The small shops in the **Yu Garden Bazaar** specialising in kites, canes, knives, buttons, chop-sticks and fans are a sight to behold (see page 54).

## ... ROMANCE

Noisy and brash as it can be, Shanghai also knows how to set a romantic mood. Share an aromatic massage at one of the cities many spas or massage parlours (see page 74), followed by a dim sum feast (see page 50). Or take a tandem ride through the leafy lanes of the **French Concession** (see page 97), then dine *à deux* on exotic Yunnanese dishes in the moodily lit **Lost Heaven** (see page 62). To round off your day, whisk your loved one up to the **VUE** bar terrace, cuddle up on a daybed with a glass of bubbly, and take in the dreamy views (see page 144).

## ... ESCAPING THE CROWDS

Thankfully in this seething metropolis, peaceful retreats abound. Little **Jing An Park** in the heart of Shanghai is a fine spot for a stroll and some people-watching (see page 76). Set amid fragrant osmanthus trees, the pavilion teahouse of **Guilin Park** (see page 162) ranks high as a Zen-infused respite. A contemplative walk around nearby **Longhua Martyrs Memorial** (see page 159) takes in commemorative statues within a lovely manicured park. To escape Xujiahui's relentless commercial buzz, just duck inside the splendid **St Ignatius Cathedral** (see page 161).

## ... A NIGHT ON THE TOWN

Shanghai's notoriously decadent 1930s nightlife scene entered a prolonged lull following World War II and the 1949 Communist Revolution. Half a century later, in the early Noughties, bar and club culture entered a kind of baby boomer explosion – mirroring China's economic boom. Today, Shanghai's nightlife compares favourably with any hard-partying global metropolis.

Opened early in the new century, **Xintiandi** is a labyrinth of upscale bars and restaurants in refashioned heritage dwellings. Nearby, the elegant French Concession streets are dotted with casual-cool drinking spots, notably **The Apartment** and **El Coctel** on Yongfu Road (see page 91), and **Liquid Laundry** on Donghu Road. A narrow strip of Yongkang Road (see page 106) is a lively bar street offering well-priced drinks and sidewalk seating.

For stylish cocktail lounges with a terrace view, the elegant riverside **Bund** is suitably well endowed. **POP** (see page 35), **Bar Rouge** (see

page 37) and **Sir Elly's** (see page 35) at The **Peninsula Shanghai** are among the top picks, while updated retro Shanghai chic is served up at the **Long Bar** (see page 31) inside the neoclassical **Waldorf Astoria** hotel.

Across the Huangpu River in Pudong, movers and shakers ascend to **Flair**, an alfresco lounge that affords dramatic skyline panoramas from the 58th floor of the **Shanghai IFC Tower** (see page 118).

Back down to earth, live music in Shanghai tends to be of the more soulful variety; talented musicians and vocalists from both home and abroad grace the stages most nights at **House of Blues and Jazz** (see page 37), **Heyday** (see page 99) and **JZ Club** (see page 99). Weekend party people make for **M1NT** and **Unico** (see page 37) in the Bund neighbourhood.

Those more classically inclined are well served by stunning world-class performance venues, including the **Shanghai Grand Theatre** (see page 71) and **Shanghai Oriental Arts Centre** (see page 125).

## ... FAMILY FUN

A reputation for daytime consumerism and after-dark excess suggests Shanghai is not a family destination. Like everything in this constantly evolving metropolis, though, attractions for young travellers are increasingly springing up. An obvious frontrunner is the **Shanghai Disney Resort** (see page 127), which opened in Pudong in summer 2016. The Shanghai Natural History will thrill dinosaur enthusiasts of all ages, and is set in a pretty sculpture park. On a rainy day, the indoor ice rink at the **Mercedes-Benz Arena** (see page 125) in Pudong is a popular attraction, followed by a visit to the **China Art Museum** (see page 121) at the 2010 World Expo Site, which really does look like it was made of Lego. Also east of the river is the adult-sounding but very kid-friendly **Shanghai Science and Technology Museum** (see page 126) which overlooks **Century Park** (see page 124) – a popular spot for kite flying, rollerblading and Frisbee throwing at weekends. Located by the Pudong waterside is the **Shanghai Ocean Aquarium** (see page 126) where sharks, Chinese water dragons and jellyfish hold youngsters in thrall.

Head to the **Bund Sightseeing Tunnel** (see page 33) for a kaleidoscopic, visually stimulating train ride beneath the Huangpu River. Also universally loved by children is taking the high-speed lift up the **Oriental Pearl Tower** (see page 122) or **Shanghai Tower** (see page 114).

## ... HISTORIC ARCHITECTURE

After Shanghai was forcibly opened up as an international port following the 1840–42 Sino-British Opium War, foreign developers set to work. The constructive legacy of 19th- and early 20th-century British, French and American domination is evident citywide. Most evocative are the neo-classical mansions of the **Bund** (see page 28) and **Rockbund** (see page 32), which hug the arcing western bank of the Huangpu River.

Head inland and **People's Square** – originally a British-built racecourse – is flanked by a handful of Art Deco gems, including some **historic hotels** (see page 73). The former **French Concession** (see pages 90 and 102) is an alluring mix of soulful architecture, ranging from Art Deco apartment residences to European villas and manor houses – many of which have been converted into bars, restaurants and boutique hotels.

North of People's Square, **Hongkou** is another district richly imbued with historic architecture, including the World War II **Jewish Ghetto** (see page 133) and **1933** (see page 134), an Art Deco abattoir turned retail and dining destination. More surprising landmarks can be admired on the **North Bank of Suzhou Creek**, just across **Waibaidu Bridge**, itself an architectural icon (see page 138).

## ... MODERN ICONS

Shanghai's name translates into English as 'Above the Sea', and staring at the cloud-level skyline, elevation is the dominant theme – especially east of the river in Pudong. Here, the **Shanghai Tower** is the world's second-tallest building. Along with the **Shanghai World Financial Centre** and **Jinmao Tower, i**t completes a triptych of super towers that dominate the Shanghai skyline (see page 114). Modern architecture blending western function and Asian influences include architect Arata Isozaki's **Himalayas Centre** (see page 123) and the Paul Andreu-designed **Oriental Art Centre** (see page 125), while the **China Art Museum** (see page 121) at the former World Expo site is a contemporary take on traditional Chinese structural design. Coming out of left-field is the oyster shell-shaped **Mercedes-Benz Arena** (see page 121) which resembles a spaceship about to take off when lit in neon at night. In Puxi, two ultra high-rise towers containing the **JW Marriott Tomorrow Square** (www.marriott.co.uk/jw-marriott) and **Le Royal Meridien Shanghai** (www.leroyalmeridien shanghai.com) dominate the 1930s Art Deco gems on People's Square. Here, too, modern architecture makes its mark in the form of the **Shanghai Grand Theatre** (see page 71) and the **Urban Planning Exhibition Centre** (see page 70).

## ... CONTEMPORARY ART

Chinese contemporary art has become one of the hottest commodities in the art world and Shanghai has cleverly combined culture with commerce to become a major art centre. The state-owned **China Art Museum** (see page 121) and **Powerstation of Art** (see page 156) showcase the world's biggest collection of modern Chinese art and contemporary art, respectively. The West Bund Cultural Corridor is home to several private museums in repurposed warehouse spaces, including a former military aircraft hangar (see page 156). A cluster of industrial buildings on **Moganshan Road** have been transformed into a funky art district where leading galleries show works by China's top artists (see page 136). West of the city centre, **Redtown** (see page 155) features sculpture, painting and photographic galleries set around a park. A concentration of small galleries can be found in the lanes of the former French Concession including the internationally minded **Art Labor** (see page 107).

The **Rockbund Art Museum** (see page 32) in a renovated 1930s building behind the Bund, and **Shanghai MOCA** (see page 68) in the heart of People's Park are great artsy stops in popular tourist areas. Further afield in Baoshan, the superbly curated **Shanghai Museum of Glass** (see page 135) more than merits the journey.

## ... BEING PAMPERED

Shanghai's high-octane moneymakers and office toilers rebalance their in-ner calm with a relaxing back or foot rub. As a result, most streets feature a (legal) massage parlour and/or a full-service urban spa. Locally based mid-range spa chain **Dragonfly** (see page 74) has multiple branches offering Chinese and aroma massages and facials. Another popular, value-for-money chain, **Green Massage** (see page 74), offers a comprehensive

menu of regular massages along with Traditional Chinese Medicine (TCM) therapies, such as ear candling and cupping, that have been used for cen-turies to balance the body and spirit. **Anantara Spa** (see page 74) at The Puli Hotel & Spa draws local inspiration from the healing power of Chinese tea. For the ultimate wellness high, take the elevator to the 53rd floor of Pudong's **IFC Shanghai tower** (see page 118). Here, the **Ritz-Carlton Spa by ESPA** is a sumptuous sky-high retreat offering massages, facials and body wraps, plus an infinity swimming pool yielding dramatic city panora-mas. Take a dip into traditional **Chinese bathhouse culture**, for a unique, if somewhat stripped down, wellness experience (see page 152).

## ... LOCAL CUISINE

Shanghai reads like a culinary map of the nation. For delicious *xiaolongbao* dumplings, try Taiwanese chain **Din Tai Fung** (see page 120), or hearty Shengjian dumplings at **Yang's Fry Dumpling** (see page 75). **Nanling** (see page 101) and **Shanghai Min** (see page 120) serve tasty renditions of local Shanghainese cuisine. **Sichuan Citizen** (see page 100) heats things up with peppery hotpots, while **Lost Heaven** (see page 62) fuses Yunnan, Thai and Burmese flavours. Far-west Xinjiang province is represented at **Xibo** (see page 100), while exotic street food from this region is also on offer at the **Friday Muslim Market** (see page 141). Avid chefs can learn to prepare Chinese dishes at a **local cooking school** (see page 105).

## ... LITERARY INSPIRATION

In its 1930s heyday, Shanghai was the heart of China's literary scene, and it remains an important centre even with today's heavily censored media. North of downtown, **Duolun Road** (see page 132) has many restored houses and cafés frequented by Shanghai's pre-War literati. At the quaint **Old China Hand Reading Room** (see page 96) you can browse fascinating tomes while sipping tea. Host venue for the annual Shanghai International Literary Festival, **Glam** (see page 38) also presents afternoon talks by authors.

# NEIGHBOURHOODS

The limits of this maritime city are defined by its waterways. The Huangpu River separates Shanghai's newest district, Pudong in the east, from the rest of Shanghai, known as Puxi, to the west. The Suzhou Creek divides the thriving midsection of Puxi from its quieter northern suburbs. New lines have been drawn, but the shape and feel of the old foreign Concessions and Nanshi – the Old Chinese City – are still discernible. Shanghai streets run north to south and east to west in grid-like fashion, except for oval-shaped Nanshi and People's Square, the latter defined by the old racetracks.

**The Bund and Huangpu.** Shanghai's most celebrated strip of historic real estate is the Bund, which stretches for one mile along the west bank of the Huangpu River. Here, stately Concession-era buildings have been converted into hotels, restaurants, banks and boutiques. The intriguing streets and lanes behind the Bund are filled with fine architecture and the enduring aura of Old Shanghai.

**Xintiandi, Yu Garden and South Bund.** Southwest of the Bund, Xintiandi (meaning 'New Heaven and Earth') is a two-block area of refurbished *shikumen* or lane houses, filled with boutiques, restaurants and bars. To the east, this buzzing shopping and nightlife enclave segues into Nanshi – the Old Chinese City around Yu Garden – and the South Bund.

**People's Square and Jing'an.** The People's Square area is the city's geographical centre, its oval shape delineated by the former British-built racetrack. The old Jockey Club and leafy People's Park stand alongside thought-provoking contemporary landmarks including the Urban Planning Exhibition Hall, Shanghai Grand Theatre and Shanghai Museum, forming a hotchpotch landscape framed by soaring mega-towers. Several of Shanghai's main metro lines converge at this vast square, transporting people from all over the city to its cultural and political hub.

**Former French Concession.** In the mid-19th century, Shanghai was carved into self-governing 'concessions' by the dominant British, American and French powers. The former French Concession, south of what is today's Yan'an Elevated Highway, became the city's most architecturally rich district, with European villas, Art Deco residences and plane trees flanking the French-named avenues. Today, these elegant streets boast some of Shanghai's most charming restaurants, cafés and drinking spots.

**Pudong.** Until the 1990s, the vast tract of land east of the Huangpu River was a sparsely populated area of marshland. Fast-forward to today and Pudong epitomises futuristic Shanghai. The riverside Lujiazui district is home to China's financial centre, one of its two stock exchanges and some of its tallest skyscrapers. Beyond is a sprawling residential and retail landscape including glitzy malls, Shanghai Disney Resort and China's second-busiest airport.

**Suzhou Creek and the Northern Districts.** North of People's Square are the rapidly gentrifying districts around Suzhou Creek. Former factories and warehouses of this old industrial zone are being converted into hip museums, galleries and artists' studios. The forgotten district around Jiangwan Stadium is an impressive legacy of attempts by Chiang Kai-shek's Nationalists to build a new city on Shanghai's fringes.

**Xujiahui, Changning and Hongqiao.** These adjacent western districts span the thriving mall scene and historic attractions of Xujiahui, the high-rise hotels and high-speed railway hub of Hongqiao and the western extremity of the French Concession. Awaiting discovery is an eclectic mix of sculpture gardens, Japanese and Korean cuisine, a Gothic cathedral and an exquisitely landscaped park.

YICHUAN

YANGJIAQIAO

Yuling

ZHENRU

Shanghai Huochezhan
(Shanghai Railway Station)

MENGQING
GONGYUAN

ZHUJIAWAN

M50

CHANGSHOU
GONGYUAN

Suzhou Creek

Yu Fo Si
(Jade Buddha Temple)

JING AN

Xin Guang

Wusong

RENMIN GONGYUAN
(PEOPLE'S PARK)

Shanghai
Shangcheng
(Shanghai Centre)

Shanghai Renmin Zhengfu
(City Hall)

ZHONGSHAN
GONGYUAN

Shanghai Bowuguan
(Shanghai Museum)

Jingan Si
(Jing An Temple)

Shanghai Zhanlan
Zhongxin
(Shanghai
Exhibition Centre)

Shang Xia

ZHOUJIAQIAO

Shi Shaonian Gong
(Municipal Children's Palace/Marble Hall)

JINGAN
GONGYUAN

Xintiandi

XIANGYANG
GONGYUAN

FUXING
GONGYUAN

TAIPINGQIAO
GONGYUAN

Zhongguo Lanyin
Huabu Guan
(Chinese Printed Blue
Nankeen Exhibition Hall)

Sun Zhongshan Gu
(former Residence o
Sun Yat-sen)

DINGXIANG
HUAYUAN

FRENCH
CONCESSION

Wenhua Guangchang
(Cultural Square)

Zhou Enlai Guju
(former residence o
Zhou Enlai)

Mary Ching
& Leo Gallery

Shanghai Tushuguan
(Shanghai Library)

Jiashan
Market

Tianzifang

HONGQIAO

CHANGNING

Guojie Jiaotang
(Shanghai
International
Community Church)

Zhongguo Gongchandang
Shanghai Shi Wei Yuanhui
(Communist Party HQ)

XUJIAHUI
GONGYUAN

Hongqiao International
Airport

DAPUQIAO

Soong Qingling's
Mausoleum

Bibliotheca
Zikawei

Nanpu
Railway
Station

XUHUI

Dapu Road
Tunnel

MINHANG

Shanghai Botanical Garden

Shanghai Museum of Glass

LUXUN
GONGYUAN
HONGKOU

HEPING
GONGYUAN

Yangshupu

YANGPU

Duolun Road

Huoshan
Park

SICHUAN
NORTH ROAD
GONGYUAN

1933

Youtairen Zai Shanghai Jinianguan
(Jewish Refugees Museum)

Yangpu
Bridge

International
Cruise Terminal

Xinjian
Road
Tunnel

Dalian
Road
Tunnel

Huangpu

JINGNAN

Broadway
Mansions

Waibaidu
Bridge

Bund
Sightseeing
Tunnel

Dongfang Mingzhu
Guangbo Dianshi Ta
(Oriental Pearl Tower)

No.'s 33-53
Waitan Yuan
former
British Consulate

The Bund

LUJIAZUI
GONGYUAN

MEIYUAN

Suzhou

UANGPU

Zhen Da Guangchang
(Super Brand Mall)

Jinmao Dasha
(Jinmao Tower)

PUDONG

Yan'an Road
Tunnel

Shanghai Tower
(under construction)

No.3 Three on
the Bund

Remin Road
Tunnel

Dongfang Yishu Zhongxin
(Oriental Art Centre)

GUCHENG
GONGYUAN

Nanxiang

Chenghuang Miao
(City Temple of Shanghai)

WEIFANG

NANSHI

Xiaofaoyuan Qingzhensi
(Peach Orchard Mosque)

Fuxing Road
Tunnel

LAOXIMEN

Wen Miao
(Confucius Temple)

Shanghai Kejiguan
(Shanghai Science and
Technology Museum)

SHIJI
GONGYUAN
(CENTURY
PARK)

Body & Soul
Clinic

DONGJIADU

South Bund
Fabric Market

HUANGPU

Nanpu
Bridge

HUAMUZHEN

Longyang Road Station
(Maglev)

Minjian Shouzanpin
Chenliequan
(Museum of Folk Art)

LONGYANG

LINYU

Xizang Road
Tunnel

Bailian

Shanghai

N

Lupu
Bridge

Huangpu

0    200   400   600   800   1000 yds

OUTAN
NGYUAN

Mercedes-Benz Arena

0   200   400   600   800   1000 m

World Expo
Site

China Pavilion

# THE BUND AND HUANGPU

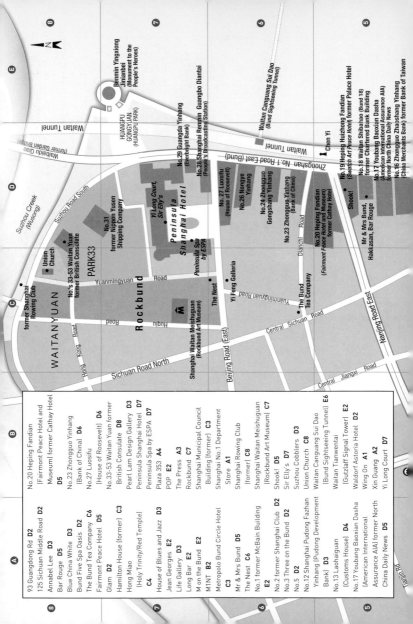

**WAITANYUAN**

**PARK33**

Suzhou Creek (Wusong)

Suzhou Road South

former Shanghai
Rowing Club

Union
Church

No.'s 33-53 Waitan Yuan
former British Consulate

No.31
former Nippon Yusen
Shipping Company

Yuanmingyuan Road

**Rockbund**

Huqiu Road

Hong Kong Road

Yi Long Court,
Sir Elly's

**Peninsula
Shanghai Hotel**

Peninsula Spa
by ESPA

Yi Feng Galleria

The Nest

Shanghai Waitan Meishuguan
(Rockbund Art Museum)

Beijing Road (East)

The Bund
Tea Company

Yuanmingyuan Road

Sichuan Road North

Central Sichuan Road

Central Jiangxi Road

Nanjing Road East

Nanjing Rd

Waibaidu Qiao
(former Garden Bridge)

Waitan Tunnel

Waitan Tunnel

**HUANGPU
GONGYUAN
(HUANGPU PARK)**

**Renmin Yingxiong
Jinianbei
(Monument to the
People's Heroes)**

Waitan Canguang Sui Dao
(Bund Sightseeing Tunnel)

No.29 Guangda Yinhang
(Everbright Bank)

No.28 Shanghai Renmin Guangbo Diantai
(People's Broadcasting Station)

Zhongshan No.1 Road East (Bund)

No.27 Luosifu
(House of Roosevelt)

No.26 Nongye
Yinhang

No.24 Zhongguo
Gongshang Yinhang

No.23 Zhongguo Yinhang
(Bank of China)

Dianchi
Road

No.20 Heping Fandian
(Fairmont Peace Hotel and Museum)
former Cathay Hotel

Mr & Mrs Bund,
Hakkasan, Bar Rouge

No.19 Heping Huizhong Fandian
(Swatch Art Peace Hotel) former Palace Hotel

No.18 Waitan Shibaihao (Bund 18)
former Chartered Bank Building

No.17 Youbang Baoxian Dasha
(American International Assurance AIA)
former North China Daily News

No.16 Zhongguo Zhaoshang Yinhang
(China Merchants Bank) former Bank of Taiwan

Shook!

Chen Yi

N

# The Bund and Huangpu

Huangpu

HUANGPU 黄浦区

**Promenade**

Waitan Tunnel

Zhongshan No.1 Road East (Bund)

No.14

Jian Yi Zhongxin (Shanghai Gold Exchange) former Russo-Asiatic Bank

No.13 Laohaiguan (Customs House)

No.12 Shanghai Pudong Fazhan Yinhang (Pudong Development Bank)

No.17 former Russell & Company

Blue China White, Suzhou Cobblers, Annabel Lee and Life Gallery

No.7 Bangkok Bank

No.6

No.5 · M on the Bund, Glam

Jean Georges, Mercato, CHI-Q, POP, Unico

No.3, Three on the Bund

Long Bar

Waitan Tianwentai (Gutzlaff Signal Tower) (Bund Signal Tower)

Waldorf Astoria (No.2 former Shanghai Club)

No.1 former McBain Building

Pearl Lam Design Gallery (185 Sichuan Middle Road)

House of Blues and Jazz

Metropolo Bund Circle Hotel

former Hamilton House

Central Sichuan Road

Xinhua News Group (125 Sichuan Middle Road)

China Minsheng Bank (93 Guangdong Road)

Guangdong Road

Central Jiangxi Road

Fuzhou Road

former Shanghai Municipal Council Building

former American Club

Hong Miao (Holy Trinity/Red Temple)

Hankou Road (Hankou Lu)

Jiujiang Road (Jiujiang Lu)

Fuzhou Road

Central Henan Road (Henan Zhong Lu)

Central Shandong Road

The Press

M:NT

Yan'an Road East (Yan'an Dong Lu)

EAST NANJING RD

Nanjing Road Pedestrian Mall

Plaza 353

Jiujiang Road (Jiujiang Lu)

## Inset map

Peninsula Shanghai Hotel

Zhongshan No.1 Road (E.) (Bund)

Nanjing Road (E.)

(Beijing Donglu)

Beijing Road (E.)

Central

Central

Jiujiang Road

Hankou Road

Fuzhou Jiangxi Rd

Henan

Central

Nanjing Road

Shandong Rd

Central

Road

Yan'an Rd (E.)

Guangdong

Central

Niuzhuang Road

Tianjin

Road

Fujian

Guangdong

Zhejiang Rd

Guangdong Rd

see above

Beijing Road (E.)

Niuzhuang Road

Ningbo Road

Xin Guang · Wing On

Nanjing Road Pedestrian Mall

Central Fuzhou Rd

Zhejiang

Guangxi

Central Tibet (Xizang) Road

Shanghai No.1 Department Store

Raffles City

Guangxi Rd (N.)

Mu'en Tang (Moore Church)

**Scale bars:**

0 — 50 — 100 — 150 — 200 m
0 — 50 — 100 — 150 — 200 yds

0 — 500 m
0 — 500 yds

N

# Take a walking tour of the iconic Bund, and admire the stately colonial mansions of Old Shanghai

Known locally as Waitan (Outside Beach), the two-kilometre sweep of magnificent historic buildings west of the Huangpu River, is a Concession-era time capsule. After the end of the first Sino-British Opium War in 1842, China was forced to open up Shanghai's port to foreign trade. What was then a muddy river bank became the docking station for merchant ships. As commerce boomed, this waterfront stretch became the economic engine of the British Concession. An embankment lined with jetties was built in the late 1880s, and by the early 20th century, the Bund (from the Anglo-Indian word meaning embanked quay), backed by trading houses and the grandiose headquarters of international financial institutions, had become known as the 'Wall Street of Asia'.

Almost a century later, Shanghai's riverfront was given a multi-million dollar makeover ahead of the 2010 World Expo. Traffic lanes were rerouted underground, the riverside boardwalk was broadened, new public spaces were created, and the iconic buildings were sand-blasted and endowed with beautiful new lighting.

### A walk along the bund
Starting at the southern end of the Bund, the first building is the neoclassical **McBain Building** (No.1),

built in 1915 and formerly the HQ of a shipping magnate. The elegant 1911 building at No.2, once occupied by the exclusive Shanghai Club, is now the glitzy **Waldorf Astoria hotel**, home to the legendary Long Bar (see page 31). Next door, the former **Union Assurance Building** (No.3) is one of nine neoclassical buildings designed by British architects, Palmer & Turner. Now named **Three on the Bund**, it houses the gourmet temples of Jean Georges Vongerichten (see page 34) among other restaurants, nightclubs and fashion boutiques. At No.5, the former Nissin Kisen Kaisha Shipping Building is now occupied by high-end restaurants, most notably **M on the Bund** restaurant (see page 34) and the cool lounge, **Glam** (see page 38).

Heading up the Bund, you'll come to two of its most iconic buildings. The palatial **Shanghai Pudong Development Bank** (No. 12) was designed by Palmer & Turner as the HQ for the Hong Kong and Shanghai bank. When completed in 1921, it was hailed as 'the finest building east of the Suez'. Inside, the cavernous marble lobby features a cupola mosaic depicting images of the eight global cities in which the bank then operated. Opened in 1927, the neighbouring **Custom House** (No. 13) is another Palmer & Turner gem. The bronze bas relief in the entrance lobby depicts heroic revolution symbolically set in front of the foreign-built Bund. The clock tower, fondly referred to as 'The Big Ching', was modelled on London's Big Ben. The American International Assurance or AIA building at No. 17 was the Bund's tallest when it was completed in 1923 as the **North China Daily News HQ.** The oldest and most influential newspaper of the time operated here from 1864 to 1951. The lobby is open during office hours, so be sure to take a peek at its interior. Past the iconic **Peace Hotel** at No. 20 (see page 30), the slim **Bank of China** (No. 22), another Palmer & Turner creation, is a harmonious blend of Chinese, classical and Art Deco themes (open during working hours). Built in 1922, the granite-clad **House of Roosevelt** at No. 27, formerly the Jardine Matheson building, was one of the great trading houses of Concession-era Shanghai. It is now a collection of bars, restaurants and shops.

The last buildings on the Bund are the oldest. Built in 1873, Nos. 33–53 were occupied by the former **British Consulate**. The buildings are off limits but the spectacular grounds are open to the public (see page 32).

## Saunter through the hallowed halls of the Peace Hotel and listen to its octogenarian jazz band

The Shanghai landscape owes considerable thanks to Sir Victor Sassoon. During the 1920s and '30s, the flamboyant financier and scion of the great opium-trading firm, E.D. Sassoon, built several of the city's finest buildings, including Hamilton House, Metropole Hotel, Cathay Cinema, Cathay Mansions and the Embankment Building. The tycoon's most prized legacy, however, is Sassoon House, known today as the **Fairmont Peace Hotel**. When it opened in 1929, Sassoon House incorporated the ultra-luxurious

Cathay Hotel on its fourth to seventh floors. China's finest hotel fast became a legend in a city of legends. From day one, the sleek, Art Deco building crowned by a green copper pyramid was the social centre of Shanghai. Business leaders, celebrities, gangsters and the social elite partied in the sprung wooden ballroom and luxuriated in hotel rooms with previously unseen luxuries such as air conditioning, Lalique glass detailing, marble bathrooms and silver coffee pots. Noel Coward, Charlie Chaplin and George Bernard Shaw all checked in during its heyday.

Following much needed renovations, Shanghai's most iconic hotel reopened in 2010. The second-floor Peace Museum tells compelling stories, through photos and hotel artefacts, including serving spoons and crystal goblets engraved with the Cathay Hotel logo of the 'Claridges of the East' and its benefactor.

For a musical meander down memory lane, the vintage jazz band (all members are aged 70+) still plays timeless tunes each evening in the **Jazz Bar**.

*Fairmont Peace Hotel; 20 Nanjing Road East; tel: 6321 6888; www.fairmont.com/ peacehotel; map D5*

# Prop up the legendary Long Bar and imbibe some 1930s glamour at the Waldorf Astoria Shanghai

As a coastal city built on shipping wealth, Shanghai quickly developed a taste for waterside tippling. Few venues are more redolent of its formative drinking days than the old Shanghai Club.

Renowned in the 1920s and '30s as the most elitist social institution in Shanghai's International Concession, the Club was housed in a neoclassical Bund mansion fronted by dramatic arched windows and Corinthian columns. Inside, gentlemen of wealth and rank (it was out of bounds to everyone else) imbibed at the 33-metre (100ft) **Long Bar** and puffed Cuban cigars beneath humming ceiling fans.

The pre-war Japanese invasion of Shanghai shuttered the Club, but its legend lived on through the building's post-war days as the International Seamen's Club, a sleazy casino and China's first KFC branch.

In late 2010, the Shanghai Club legend was revived. Following three years of renovations, No.2 the Bund was reopened as the lavish Waldorf Astoria Shanghai on the Bund. Standing proud amid the hotel's Sicilian marble columns and patina marble floors is the modern incarnation of the famed Long Bar.

Re-created using historic photos and architectural drawings, the

Long Bar is outfitted with Jacobean wood panelling and backlit liquor cabinets. The replica bar – once the longest in Asia – features carved insignia and a white marble counter. Studded leather armchairs, Art Deco lamps, and sepia-tinted photos of Old Shanghai complete the nostalgic picture.

So, do as the bank managers and taipans once did. Sink into an armchair, sip a Pink Gin and relax in one of Asia's most fabled drinking establishments.

*The Long Bar; Waldorf Astoria Shanghai on the Bund, 2 Zhongshan No. 1 Road East; tel: 6322 9988; www.waldorfastoria shanghai.com; daily 2pm–1am; map D2*

# Peruse the born-again Rockbund district, stopping in at the Rockbund Art Museum

Waitanyuan – meaning 'headstream of the Bund' – lies behind the northern sweep of the Bund where Suzhou Creek meets the Huangpu River. This long-neglected historic area has undergone a long-term urban renewal project under the guidance of British starchitect David Chipperfield and its grand edifices are gradually reopening as luxury residences, offices, shops, hotels and museums.

The centerpiece of the six-acre Rockbund project is a clutch of heritage buildings between Yuanmingyuan Road and Huqiu Road, running parallel to the Bund. First to open was the **Rockbund Art**

**Museum** in the revamped former Royal Asiatic Society building, which dates from 1932. The six-floor Art Deco gallery hosts regular art, installation and photography exhibitions and has a cute terrace on the top floor serving free espressos.

A line of restored buildings strung along the pedestrianised Yuanmingyuan Road date from between 1924 and 1933. These eclectic facades feature bold Art Deco and neoclassical styling and unique Chinese influences.

Directly opposite are the grounds of the former British Consulate, accessible from the Bund side (ignore the severe looking guards – it is actually a public park). Although the residences, now private clubs and event venues, are off limits, the gardens are delightful to stroll in and are home to several century-old trees. As you swing around to the main Bund promenade, note the former **Shanghai Rowing Club** dating from 1904, offset by spectacular views of Art Deco monoliths on the opposite bank of Suzhou Creek (see page 138).

*Rockbund Art Museum; 20 Huqiu Road; tel: 3310 9985; www.rockbundartmuseum. org; Tue–Sun 10am–6pm; charge; map C7*

# Experience a trippy underwater voyage through the Bund Sightseeing Tunnel or take a public ferry

There are a number of ways to cross the Huangpu River, but the Bund Sightseeing Tunnel is undoubtedly the wackiest. The tunnel runs from beneath the promenade opposite No.27 on the Bund, exiting at the Oriental Pearl Tower on the Lujiazui bankside. The capsule ride takes passengers on a visual journey from the earth's molten core to outer space. Add a few LED screens, some flashing Christmas lights, balloon dolls and sound effects and you've got Shanghai's most kitsch tourist experience. The ride along the riverbed in air-conditioned glass capsules only takes a few minutes. It's transparently low-tech but oddly mind-altering nonetheless. Overpriced at RMB50, it nevertheless beats the grinding traffic or packed subway crossing options at peak hours.

Another fun way to cross the river is via the local ferry services that thread between the barge traffic on the busy Huangpu. There are numerous lines and stops along the river, but the most convenient stretch runs between the Shiliupu dock at the south end of the Bund and Dongchang Road in Pudong. The trip is a bargain at RMB2. Have your camera ready because the views on the short 10-minute crossing are spectacular.

*Bund Sightseeing Tunnel; 300 Zhongshan No. 1 Road East; tel: 5888 6000; daily 8am–10.30pm; map E6*

## Sample Shanghai fine dining at the waterfront's gourmet hotspots

As Shanghai's culinary reputation diversifies, and international and local chefs raise the creativity quotient, The Bund has become the city's most fashionable dining destination. **M on the Bund** (7/F, 20 Guangdong Road; tel: 6350 9988; www.m-restaurantgroup.com; map E2) kick-started smart Bund dining back in 1999. Today, it retains its A-list status thanks to a large menu of seasonal and steadfast modern European, Middle Eastern and Australian favourites, including slowly baked, salt-encased leg of lamb doused with Syrian spices, and the famed M pavlova. Book well in advance for Sunday brunch on the riverfront terrace.

Culinary celebrity Jean Georges Vongerichten opened his first restaurant outside New York at **Three on the Bund** (17 Guangdong Road; tel: 6321 7733; www.threeonthe bund.com; map D2) in 2004. The updated 1920s decor, seasonally-focused menus and 500-label wine list quickly established a loyal following. He has since expanded his Shanghai empire in the same building with the outrageously popular modern Italian, **Mercato** (tel: 6321 9922) and **CHI-Q** (tel: 6321 6622), a sleek Korean barbecue restaurant founded in partnership with his Korean wife.

At **Mr & Mrs Bund** (6/F, 18 Zhong-shan No. 1 Road East; tel: 6323 9898; www.mmbund.com; map D5) French chef Paul Pairet steers the menu between modern European and molecular gastronomy. His inventiveness attracts a hipster/foodie crowd with dishes like duck foie gras mousse with raisin hazelnut crumble. The upbeat interiors, river views and late-night supperclub menu at weekends add extra levity.

Downstairs in the same building, **Hakkasan** (tel: 6321 5888) brings modern Cantonese by way of London to Shanghai. Weekend (Fri–Sun) dim sum lunch is particularly popular, and be sure to have a pre- or post-dinner drink at the little bar in the back boasting dazzling views of the river and neon-lit skytowers.

# Don designer shades and drink in the views from the Bund's finest rooftop terraces

Many of the historic mansions along the Bund were built with sweeping stone balconies and rooftop terraces for their occupants to enjoy the sunshine and views of jetties and junks working the river. Today, the postcard-perfect backdrop of thrusting glass towers on the Pudong river bank offsets views of the waterway action.

On the top floor of **Three on the Bund** (17 Guangdong Road; tel: 6321 0909; www.threeonthebund. com; map D7) – which sports a slinky, Michael Graves-designed interior behind its stern neoclassical facade – **POP's** seventh-storey terrace is one of the Bund's finest. The wraparound verandah, adorned with potted palms and an outdoor cocktail bar, takes in the curvature of the Bund to the north and the entire Pudong skyline. For an extra-exclusive perch, book a table for two in the private stone cupola.

Opened in 2011, the **Swatch Art Peace Hotel** (23 Nanjing Road East; tel: 2329 8522; www.shook restaurantshanghai.com; map D5) revitalised the stately Edwardian Palace Hotel at the centre of the Bund. Climb to the top of the antique staircase to drink in grandstand sixth-floor river views from the large alfresco rooftop lounge.

At the north end of the Bund, the stone edifice of the **Peninsula Shanghai** (32 Zhongshan No. 1 Road East; tel: 2327 6756; www. peninsula.com; map D7) is half-a-century younger than its grandee neighbours but has continued the timeless tradition of incorporating a fine riverfront terrace. Ascend the illuminated staircase of **Sir Elly's** through the Mediterranean restaurant and step out to breathtaking 14th-floor vistas of the Bund and Pudong from the stepped rooftop lounge.

# Pick up classy local designer souvenirs at a clutch of unique Bund boutiques

Giorgio Armani pioneered luxury Bund-front shopping with his flagship boutique at Three on the Bund in 2004. Most of the luxury brand shopping can now be found in The Peninsula Arcade, home to more than 25 international brands, along with adjacent Yifeng Galleria, in a stately 1911 brick mansion. Between all this bling, a clutch of local designers' boutiques tucked away in the alleys offer some of Shanghai's most delightful souvenir hunting.

At **Blue China White**, craftsmen create hand-cast and painted porcelain fired in the ancient imperial kilns of Jingdezhen. The tableware and one-off furniture pieces have a smart, modern aesthetic and often incorporate bamboo or antique woods. Next door, **Suzhou Cobblers** is the go-to spot for traditional handmade silk slippers and totes. Inspired by 1930s Shanghai, designer Denise Huang has revived this classic footwear with updated colours and hand-embroidered motifs, like mandarin ducks, plum blossoms and pom-poms. There are also retro handbags and silk lanterns.

Tucked away down Lane 8, behind a large red door, **Annabel Lee**'s elegant showroom displays a range of quality embroidered silk pouches, cushions, shawls, jewellery and leisurewear using classic Chinese leitmotifs. Next door, Ruyee **Life Gallery** sells filmy-soft cashmere from Inner Mongolia. Along with chic adults and children's clothing and home accessories, they sell cashmere travel sets with blanket, eye mask and neck pillow, ideal for stylish jetsetters.

*Blue China White; Rm 103, 17 Fuzhou Road; map D3*
*Suzhou Cobblers; Rm 101; 17 Fuzhou Road; tel: 6321 7087; www.suzhou-cobblers.com; map D3*
*Annabel Lee; No. 1, Lane 8, Zhongshan No. 1 Road East; map D3*
*Ruyee Life Gallery; No. 2, Lane 8, Zhongshan No. 1 Road East; tel: 6301 5585; map D3*

# Party into the night at a sky-high dance club, retro jazz bar or chilled vodka lounge

As the neon skyline ignites each evening, so does the nightlife in bars and clubs across town. **Bar Rouge** (7/F, Bund 18, tel: 6339 1199; map D5) draws the late-night crowds with a heady mix of DJ beats, flamboyant cocktails and loads of attitude. A seventh-floor terrace yields super views of the Bund and the glittering Pudong skyline.

One block back from the Bund, **M1NT** (24/F, 318 Fuzhou Road; tel: 6391 28116; www.m1ntglobal.com; map B2) bills itself as a private club, but most nights it is possible to slink into this cavernous venue that draws visiting celebs and local party folk alike. Occupying the entire 24th floor penthouse of a modern skytower, the 360-degree views of Shanghai by night are matched by an equally dazzling interior of chain mail curtains, saucy murals and a vast tank filled with black and white reef-tip sharks. A roster of DJs keeps the dance floor heaving on Thursday, Friday and Saturday nights. For more chilled lounging, head to the cocktail bar or alfresco rooftop.

The **House of Blues and Jazz** (60 Fuzhou Road; map D3) recalls Shanghai's 1930s Jazz Age. In a beautifully restored heritage villa behind the Bund, retired TV and radio personality Lin Dongfu has revived the Art Deco ambience and syncopated soundtrack of his youth. Expect fat cigars, stiff G&Ts and a musical roster of top jazz and blues bands from the international circuit.

Chill lounge club **The Nest** (6/F, Rockbund, 130 Beijing East Road; map C6), a collaboration with French vodka brand Grey Goose, is a see-and-be-seen spot to kick back on low-slung 1960s-inspired designer lounges and sip vodka cocktails accompanied by fresh-shucked oysters and Nordic-inspired plates.

# Catch a chamber recital, literary conversation or cabaret act at Glam

Shanghai is no stranger to elegant cocktail lounges serving glamorous drinks at high prices. But appealing to the hip set was only ever part of **Glam**'s appeal. The Bund-front pioneer has always set itself more diverse aims, and functions as an unofficial cultural centre as well as a glam nightspot.

By the same team as M on the Bund on the same floor, credited with pioneering the renaissance of upscale dining on the Bund since 1999, Glam has had several manifestations (and names) over the years. As Glamour Bar, it occupied the entire downstairs floor until rising Bund rents forced its relocation to the original space beside the restaurant. The new name and intimate space was accompanied by a seductive new design, dressed in rich gem tones inspired by the peacock's tail and eclectic contemporary art from the owner's collection, and framed by Bund views.

Beyond the glamour, however, is real substance. Since 2003, the venue has organised and hosted the annual Shanghai International Literary Festival, the first of its kind in the city. The event, usually held in March, attracts high-calibre writers such as Andre Brink, Thomas Keneally, Gore Vidal, Su Tong, Amy Tan, Arundhati Roy and Jan Morris. Through the year, Glam's regular programme of author and historian talks and community workshops are enjoyed by a large crowd over tea and nibbles.

Eclecticism is another Glamour byword. Its cultural offerings extend to monthly chamber music concerts and the occasional avant-garde burlesque cabaret or gospel choir performance. This truly is a cultural heavyweight and glamour kitten rolled into one.

*Glam; 7/F, No. 5 The Bund (entrance on Guangdong Road); tel: 6329 3751; www.m-restaurantgroup.com/glam; daily 5pm–late; map D2*

# Take a tea break in an historic tea-trading house at The Bund Tea Company

Set back from the Bund on a quiet street corner, the Gibb, Livingston & Co. building dating from 1908 is somewhat rundown today, but still bears its gracious history and Queen Anne Revival style architectural detailing. On the ground floor, in a high-ceilinged tea salon, The Bund Tea Company pays homage to the building's original tenants and their story of tea exporting from Shanghai over 100 years ago.

Founded by two Scotsmen in 1836, Gibb, Livingston & Co imported British cotton and wool to China and in turn, exported Chinese tea and silk. They were the second trading company to open for business in the British Concession after the Shanghai port was opened to international trade, and their high-speed tea clippers often won the races between China and London to deliver the fresh tea harvest.

With its cool clipper-inspired logo and sleek packaging, the tea brand stocks an extensive selection of premium Chinese black, pu-erh, oolong, green, jasmine and white tea leaves with samples so you can take a whiff. The Shanghai sampler packs make good gifts to bring home, or take a seat in the old-world salon and enjoy a carefully steeped infusion. Note the heritage tea leaf patterns on the building façade and the mulberry leaf and silkworm cocoon motifs on the high ceilings, vestiges of Shanghai's trading history.

*The Bund Tea Company; 100 Dianchi Road; tel: 6329 0989; www.bundtea.com; map C6*

## Take in a Shanghai movie and see the Bund of yesteryear in one of its many starring roles

Ever since the first talkies were produced, Shanghai has been used as an exotic backdrop for films, and its name has featured in countless movie titles; *Shanghai Love*, *Exiled to Shanghai*, *Incident in Shanghai*, *Shadows over Shanghai*, *Shanghai Madness*, *Shanghai Gesture* and *Shanghai Express* were all big hits in the 1930s and '40s. Four decades later, Madonna failed to reprise the genre in *Shanghai Surprise* (1986). Zhang Yimou's *Shanghai Triad* (1995) was far more authentic, and Wang Ziaoshuai's *Shanghai Dreams* won the Prix du Jury at the 2005 Cannes film festival.

The Bund makes several appearances in Steven Spielberg's *Empire of the Sun*, an adaptation of JG Ballard's memoir of his school days in Japanese-occupied Shanghai. The opening scene was filmed at the Holy Trinity church just behind the Bund (see page 43), and another memorable scene shows then-child actor Christian Bale staring out from the Peace Hotel. While filming *The White Countess* (2004), which starred Ralph Fiennes and the late Natasha Richardson, Merchant Ivory brought black vintage cars, Sikh police officers and fedora hats back to several locations on the Bund. *The Painted Veil,* a period drama based on Somerset Maugham's novel, features a CGI-enhanced image of the Bund and Huangpu River. More recently, the riverside featured in the hit Bond movie *Skyfall*, in 2012.

### Shanghai cinemas

Despite the preponderance of cheap counterfeit DVDs, cineplexes continue to be popular in Shanghai. Most Chinese films are shown without subtitles. Hollywood blockbusters (often censored) are screened in English only at selected cinemas – see www.cityweekend.com.cn. The Royal Asiatic Society (www.royalasiaticsociety.org.cn) occasionally screens vintage Chinese movies.

# Climb the Bund Signal Tower for an unusual coffee or cocktail break

The striking russet-and-white striped Signal Tower at the southern end of The Bund was erected in 1907 as part of a weather warning system set up by French Jesuits (the tower was originally named the Gutzlaff Tower, after a German missionary).

Considered the starting point of the Bund, it replaced an earlier signal station on the same site dating from 1884. Its 31-metre (100ft) semaphore tower served as a control and weather station and time marker for Huangpu River traffic as well as residents across the city. A lucky survivor of the 1993 widening of Zhongshan Road, the structure was carefully hauled 20 metres (65ft) to its present site, right in the middle of the pedestrian promenade.

You can explore the interiors of this Art Nouveau landmark, now transformed into a small exhibition hall. The ground floor walls display black and white archival pictures of the Bund through the ages. A narrow spiral staircase leads to a rooftop terrace below the mast.

The upper levels are sometimes opened as a café and bar. If open, it's a charming spot to take a break on a sunny day, watching barges course up and down the river, passengers pouring on and off the ferry and streams of pedestrians pose for pictures along the Bund from this well-placed signal perch.

*1 Zhongshan No. 2 Road; tel: 3313 0871; daily noon–2am; map E2*

# Explore the atmospheric backstreets of the Bund

The bustling streets behind the Bund are some of the most thrillingly atmospheric in the city. The avenues and lanes between Henan Road and the Bund rival the riverfront for architectural drama, but are generally in a more original, ungentrified state.

Behind the Waldorf Astoria hotel, the neoclassical gem at **93 Guangdong Road** (map D2) is one of this area's finest. Dating from 1910, its original interiors are even more spectacular. It is possible to peek through the glass doors at the grand, Byzantine-style entrance foyer.

Continue north along Sichuan Road, watching out for the mad motorcyclists that career along this stretch. At **125 Sichuan Middle Road** (map D2) the headquarters of the Xinhua News Group occupies a grandiose, if dilapidated, Neoclassical mansion from 1922. Much of the Baroque detailing on the facade was lost during the Cultural Revolution

and in its place were written slogans extolling the virtues of Maoism. Although most of these revolutionary reminders are gone, if you look carefully you can still see the outline of the characters on the upper storeys.

Turn left onto Fuzhou Road and you'll soon come to a crossroads. Four stony heritage frontages encircle the intersection of Fuzhou Road and Jiangxi Road (map C3), including the almost identical facades of **Hamilton House** and the former **Metropole Hotel** (now the Metropolo Bund Circle hotel).

At 185 Sichuan Middle Road, the **Pearl Lam Design gallery** (tel: 3307 0838; www.pearllam.com; map D3) showcases cutting-edge Chinese art.

Continue north on Jiangxi Road, following the wall of the Renaissance-style **Shanghai Municipal Council building** (map C3), opened in 1922 and encompassing an entire city block. This was the seat of authority during the days of the British Concession. Great archival photos of the building hang in the entrance.

Stop for dumplings and tea at the little local stalls that line the backstreets. Alternatively, continue to **The Press** (309 Hankou Road; tel: 5169 0777; map B3); located in a 1872 mansion, for coffee and cake beneath a domed plaster ceiling.

# Go on a mini pilgrimage to historic places of Christian worship

Designed in the 1920s by Hungarian architect Ladislaus Hudec, Moore Church on People's Square was the first church in Shanghai to reopen post-Cultural Revolution (1979). Shanghai's largest Christian church open for worship is the ivy-covered Community Church on Hengshan Road, built in 1924. Both draw large congregations to their weekly services.

Shanghai in the early 20th century was the archetypal Sin City. One preacher famously declared from a Shanghai pulpit that if God allowed the city to continue to exist, 'He owed an apology to Sodom and Gomorrah'. For those seeking redemption from Shanghai's wicked 1930s ways, there were over 30 churches and four synagogues around the city.

**Holy Trinity Church** was the first Anglican church in Shanghai. This Victorian Gothic masterpiece, known locally as the Red Church on account of its ochre brickwork, was designed by British architect Sir George Gilbert Scott and served as a cloistered haven for British parishioners from 1869. Holy Trinity recently underwent restoration to return it to its original splendour; it remains closed to the public but you can catch a glimpse through the side gates. The 1926 Gothic Revival building behind Holy Trinity on Jiujiang Road was once the Cathedral School for British Boys attended by JG Ballard, who wrote about it in his semi-autobiographical novel *Empire of the Sun*.

On the corner of Yuangmingyuan Road and Nansuzhou Road stands the tiny **Union Church**, built in 1885 on the grounds of the former British Consulate. Freshly restored as part of the Rockbund regeneration (see page 32), it no longer serves as a church but is a popular backdrop for wedding snaps and fashion shows.

*Holy Trinity Church; corner Jiujiang Road and Jiangxi Road; map C4*

# Tuck into a crab banquet at Shanghai institution, Xin Guang

From September to January, Shanghai goes crab crazy. Hairy crabs (*da zha xie*), so named for their bristly legs and matted brown locks on the claws, are popular across Asia and the most prized come from the deep, cold waters of Yangcheng Lake, just outside Shanghai. Weighing just 180–250 grams, hairy crabs are notoriously small and difficult to eat. The Shanghainese make it a point of pride. **Xin Guang**, rather smartly, does not.

Just off Nanjing Road East, this restaurant cuts right to the chase, teasing out the delicate crabmeat and serving it – shell- and grapple-free – as a part of a multi-course menu. The tables are cramped and the courses come fast. When the crabs are in season (Sept–Jan), you're likely to see them corralled in green mesh bags on the first floor, direct from the restaurant's proprietary Yangcheng Lake nets. In today's chandelier-studded Shanghai, the 20-year old Xin Guang's low-key approach seems almost quaint.

True connoisseurs don't eat hairy crabs for the meat, which being freshwater, lacks the sweet brininess of ocean crabs. Instead, they prize the roe, a velvety orange crustacean butter, not unlike sea urchin, that lies just beneath the shell of female crabs. With the burden of actually eating a hairy crab neatly excised, the meat begins to make sense too: firm leg meat stir-fried with asparagus, for example, or a neat pile of shelled claws dipped in the region's mild brown vinegar.

There are several other courses on Xin Guang's RMB400 menu (their cheapest), but one thing you'll have to pay extra for is *huangjiu* – a sherry-like liquor which acts as a warming countermeasure to the crab meat, considered a 'cold' food by the Chinese. Order a bottle to ensure the correct balance of hot and cold.

*Xin Guang; 512 Tianjin Road; tel: 6322 3978; daily 11am–2pm, 5–9.30pm; map A2*

# Feel the consumer energy of Nanjing Road East, Shanghai's Fifth Avenue of the 1930s

Nanjing Road is Shanghai's main east-west thoroughfare. The eastern portion of this long road, running from People's Square (formerly the British racecourse) and intersecting at 90 degrees with the riverside Bund, was the hub of Shanghai commercialism during the early 1900s. Known as Shanghai's 'Fifth Avenue', it was lined with shophouses, restaurants, luxury hotels, private clubs, cinemas and the 'Big Four' department stores, each owned by overseas Chinese families.

Although Shanghai's luxury malls have now migrated to the west end, around Jing'an Temple, Nanjing Road East is still extremely popular with local tourists. On weekends and holidays, up to one million shoppers pack the pedestrianised promenade through the day and night. It really comes alive in the early evening, when the storefronts are illuminated with neon-lit Chinese signage.

Starting at the corner of Xizang Road, the commanding Art Deco **No. 1 Department Store** opened in 1936 as the exclusive Sun Department Store with the first escalator in Shanghai. At No. 635, the graceful **Wing On**, dating back to 1918, had a roof garden where guests watched Shaoxing opera. At No. 353, another heritage building is now home to an urban youth concept mall, **Plaza 353**, with a food court at the top.

The high point of any walk along Nanjing Road is the final part, where the road widens to meet the Bund. On a clear day, the view in front of the soaring Pudong skyline beyond the Huangpu River is a defining image of contemporary Shanghai.

Opened in 2011, the luxury **Swatch Art Peace Hotel** at the intersection provides more shopping opportunities for those without weary wallets. If you're in the market for a special watch, this is the place to come. The ornate ground floor of this gracious Edwardian building is given over to boutiques of prestigious brands Breguet, Blancpain, Omega and Swatch (all part of the Swatch Group). For stylish alfresco refreshment and views, finish on the sixth-floor terrace (see page 35).

*Nanjing Road East; map B5–D5*

# XINTIANDI, YU GARDEN AND SOUTH BUND

# Xintiandi, Yu Garden and South Bund

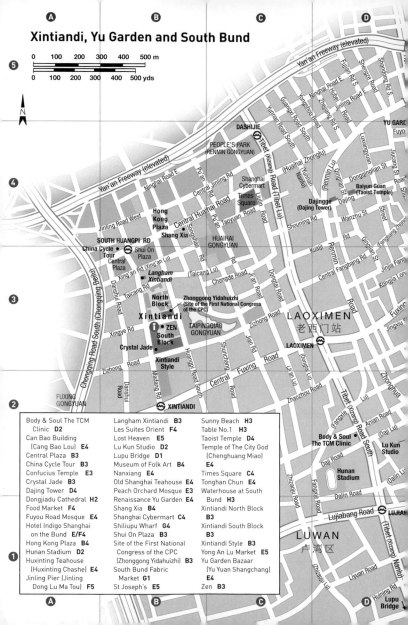

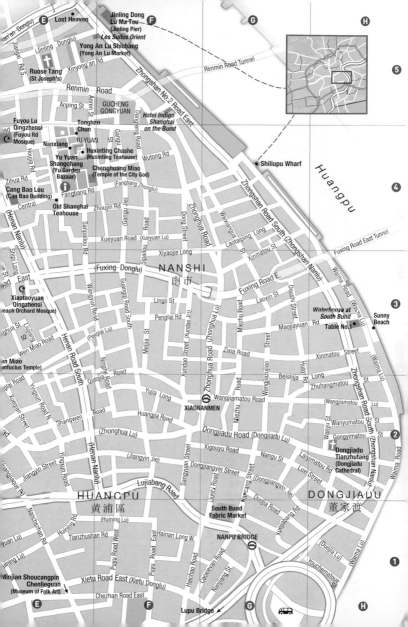

# Charge your chopsticks for a dim sum feast

Although traditionally a southern Chinese ritual, Shanghai has its own array of dim sum specialities, known as 'w' in Mandarin. These are usually eaten for breakfast or at the end of a meal. Some restaurants, however, serve both Cantonese- and Shanghai-style dim sum as a quick-fire succession of small savoury and sweet plates, accompanied by a pot of tea that is endlessly refilled.

The Shanghainese don't select their plates from carts like their Hong Kong counterparts. Instead they prefer to mark off dishes on a form and have them whisked straight from the kitchen to the table as they are ready. Among local favourites are the *xiaolongbao* (steamed pork and crabmeat soup dumplings) and the heavier *shengjian* (pan-fried dough dump-lings filled with pork, and broth). Vegetables rolled in light, crispy tofu skin *(fupi juan)* and pancakes filled with sweet date or red bean paste *(dousha bing)* are other must-try dishes.

Several restaurants in the charming grey-brick alleys of Xin-tiandi offer daily dim sum menus in smart surroundings. **Crystal Jade** is the most popular, so book ahead or be prepared to queue at week-ends as large groups of families and friends congregate over steam-ing baskets and pots of *longjing* tea. The extensive Cantonese dim sum menu is served until 3.30pm only.

**ZEN**, in a rebuilt heritage residence with soaring ceilings and lotus lamps, is a stylish affair. As the name suggests, the usual bustle and noise of the dim sum experience is replaced by a medita-tive calm. If you enjoy your dim sum dainty and exquisitely presented, ZEN is the place.

*Crystal Jade; 12A&B, 2/F, House 6–7, South Block Xintiandi, Lane 123 Xingye Road; tel: 6385 8752; Mon–Sat 11am–10.30pm, Sun 10.30am–10.30pm, dim sum service finishes at 3.30pm; map B3*
*ZEN; South Block Xintiandi, Lane 123 Xingye Road; tel: 6385 6385; daily 11am–10.30pm; map B3*

# Visit a political shrine of the Chinese Communist Party

On 1 July 2011, China staged what it called 'a birthday party for a billion people' – a nationwide celebration of the 90th anniversary of the Chinese Communist Party. Buildings were illuminated in red, groups massed in city centres singing Communist songs, and a big-budget movie featuring a roll call of China's leading stars was released showing the official version of the CPC's founding. The modern urban centres of 21st-century China in which these celebrations were set are a far cry from the humble surrounds of the First National Congress of the Communist Party of China, which took place in a small lane house in Shanghai on 23 July 1921. Mao Zedong and his fellow revolutionaries were forced to meet in this clandestine setting, and move around frequently to avoid the attentions of the authorities. Although that first Congress wasn't in fact completed here – the delegates fled when news of the illegal gathering reached the ears of the French Concession's gendarmes – this remains one of Chinese Communism's most sacred sites. The fact that it is now at the heart of the vibrant shopping and entertainment district of Xintiandi is an irony that would not have been lost

on Mao and his band of Communist missionaries.

Inside, the museum recounts the history of the Communist Party, with grainy pictures of the original delegates, film clips showing the horrors of the capitalist treatment of workers, some fine Concession-era artefacts, and a dramatic 'Last Supper' style wax-figure tableau of Mao exhorting his seated rivals over a dinner table.

*Site of the First National Congress of the Communist Party of China; 76 Xingye Road; tel: 5383 2171; daily 9am–4pm; free; map B3*

# Follow our trail for the top Xintiandi shopping picks

Whether you're looking for high fashion, souvenirs or one-off pieces by local designers, the streets around Xintiandi offer some unique shopping finds.

The grey-brick lanes of the luxury lifestyle development itself are home to designer boutiques like 'Paris of the Orient'-inspired global label **Shanghai Tang** (House 15, Xintiandi North Block, Lane 181 Taicang Road) and hipster hotspot **I.T.** (1–2/F, Building 7, Lane 123 Xingye Road). Adjoining the south block, **Xintiandi Style** mall (245 Madang Road; map B3) showcases an impressive mix of home-spun Chinese design talent and international styles. Get acquainted with Wang Yi Yang's conceptual androgyny at **Zuczug** (L204) and find stand-out-from-the-crowd tailoring and materials at **Content** (L233). Shanghai fashion designer **Uma Wang**'s flagship store (L229) is draped with gothic-inspired womenswear in sensuous fabrics such as tulle, cashmere and silk, though the spotlight belongs to her exceptional knitwear with some pieces taking weeks to hand stitch. Sartorialists will also love **Alter** (L116), a multi-brand concept store that feels like walking right into a fashion magazine. It stocks a well-edited collection of global brands, including interesting labels from Korea, plus statement jewellery and accessories.

Pretty presents for friends can be found at **Oshadai** (L232, Xintiandi Style), which stocks colourful clothing and accessories by Chinese-based French designers, and nearby at **Accent Objects** (Unit 3, Bldg 25, Lane 181 Taicang Road).

*Xintiandi: map B3*

# Lust over mod-Oriental designs made with age-old techniques at the Shang Xia boutique

Birkin Bags may be ubiquitous on the arms of Shanghai fashionistas, but French design house Hermès has gone to even greater lengths to sate the whims of its fastest-growing market. In 2010, it unveiled a new luxury brand created for and about China.

**Shang Xia** – meaning 'up down' in Mandarin – presents a contemporary take on traditional Chinese design. The label's creative director is French-trained Shanghainese designer Jiang Qiong'er, whose father designed the *ding*-shaped Shanghai Museum. She works with a variety of local artisans who handcraft her mod-classic designs according to age-old techniques. In this way Shang Xia hopes to preserve and renew endangered heritage crafts and bring back the prestige of 'Made in China'.

Shang Xia and parent brand Hermes occupy a vast three-storey redbrick maison on Huaihai Road that once housed a school. The dreamy space designed by Japanese architect Kengo Kuma is wrapped in cloud-like layers of diaphanous white tulle. Within these clouds are capsule collections of rare zitan wood furniture, fine egg-shell porcelain dishware and china tea sets encased in handwoven bamboo strands. Signature fashions include wide-sleeved gowns and coats made from hand-pulled Mongolian cashmere. There's also a jewellery range encompassing precious jades, scented antique sandalwood and auspicious charms. As you browse, assistants will conduct an in-store tea ceremony. Of course, modern Chinese luxury doesn't come cheap – prices range from RMB180–250,000.

*Shang Xia; 233 Huaihai Middle Road; tel: 8017 9777, www.shang-xia.com; daily 10am–10pm; map B4*

# Tour the Old City, from the bustling Bazaar to the traditional Ming-style Yu Garden

The original settlement of Shanghai sprang up some 2,000 years ago around the area of today's Yu Garden on the western bank of the Huangpu River. A small fishing village, it was surrounded by a 5-km (3-mile) wall built in 1553 during the Ming dynasty to ward off Japanese pirates. Only a small section of the original city wall remains, at Guchengqiang Dajingge Pavilion on Dajing Road, but you can trace the exact contours of the Old City by following the loop composed of today's Renmin Road and Zhonghua Road. Within this arc you'll find an atmospheric Chinatown dominated by wing-tipped pavilions, incense-filled temples, a bustling bazaar and traditional gardens.

Unfortunately, most of the historic buildings have been rebuilt and the area appears as a Disneyfied version of old Shanghai – with KFC, Starbucks and McDonalds competing for space with teahouses and dumpling restaurants. Nevertheless, the energy is compelling, and the streets offer vibrant insights into a side of Shanghai often lost amidst the gloss of today's globalised city.

At the heart of the Old City is Chenghuang Miao, or **Temple of the City God** (249 Fangbang Middle Road; tel: 6386 5700; daily 8.30am–4.30pm; charge; map E4). Built in 1403, it is dedicated to the gods that protect the city and its people. Worshippers and tourists crowd the complex, burning long incense sticks and bowing to the different deities representing career, family and health in the surrounding pavilions.

## Yu Garden Bazaar

Exiting the rear gate of the temple takes you into the **Yu Garden Bazaar** (map E4) – a bold and brash, vehicle-free, reinvented Ming-era Chinese experience. Delve into the frenetic corridors and browse the speciality shops selling everything from silk pyjamas, chopsticks and canes to buttons, kites, fans and scissors.

The focal point of the Bazaar is the central square where toy vendors demonstrate their wares, street performers awe the crowds, and tourists bounce along in sedan chairs. Here you'll find the **Bridge of Nine Turnings**. The zig-zag bridge is meant to ward off evil spirits, who supposedly only travel in straight lines. It leads across a carp pond to the **Huxinting Tea House**, reputedly the inspiration of the house on the Willow Pattern plate series. Queen Elizabeth II is among many VIPs who have sipped tea in this pretty pavilion.

Opposite the teahouse, a permanent queue leads to **Nanxiang restaurant** (85 Yuyuan Road; tel: 6355 4206; daily 7am–8pm; map E4), famed for its steamed pork and crabmeat soup dumplings. The upstairs rooms serve better quality (though pricier) dumplings than the takeaway window, and the wait is shorter. A more acquired taste, but much loved by locals, is stinky tofu (chou doufu). Numerous counters around the square sell these deep-fried squares of fermented tofu topped with chilli sauce.

### Yu Garden

At the north end of the bridge is **Yu Yuan** (218 Anren Road; daily 8.30am–5.30pm; charge; map E4), or Garden of Leisurely Repose. This Ming-style garden was established in 1577 as the private retreat of Sichuan Governor Pan Yunduan. Its manicured gardens, rockeries and pavilions offer an escape, of sorts (it is usually very crowded), from the madness of the Bazaar.

# Visit a traditional Chinese medicine hall for acupuncture, cupping treatments or herbal remedies

The origins of traditional Chinese medicine (TCM) can be traced back thousands of years. It is rooted in ideas of balance and harmony, yin and yang. To correct body imbalances and maintain good health, TCM prescribes physical therapies like acupuncture, tuina massage and fire cupping, plus herbal supplements and fortifying elixirs. Even the daily diet is supplemented with seasonal foods that have specific 'heating' or 'cooling' properties.

**Tonghan Chun** in the Old City bazaar, is the oldest traditional Chinese medicine shop in the city, dating back to 1783. The multi-level health emporium, styled like an ancient temple, sells a huge variety of medical supplies, including some of TCM's more exotic remedies, such as old ginseng roots costing hundreds of thousands of yuan, deer antlers and tiger penis.

The store also has a group of affiliated TCM doctors available for consultations. Diagnoses start by assessing the pulse, face, tongue and body, and also take the patient's medical history, living habits and emotional wellbeing into consideration.

If you want a professional consultation in English, **Body & Soul – The TCM Clinic** is run by TCM-trained German doctor Doris Rathgeber. Her clinic offers TCM therapies complemented with Western medical knowledge in a comforting environment. Multi-lingual physicians specialise in acupuncture, internal medicine, physiotherapy and psychological consulting, and can concoct special herbs for jet lag sufferers too.

*Tonghan Chun; 20 New Yuyuan Road; tel: 6355 0308; daily 9am–4pm; map E4*
*Body & Soul – The TCM Clinic; Suite 5, 14/F, Anji Plaza, 1 Jianguo Xin Road; tel: 5101 9262; www.bodyandsoul.com.cn; map D2*

# Rummage for antiques and Maomentos, then take tea in the delightfully retro Old Shanghai Teahouse

Shanghai antiques are prized commodities, and the streets around the Old City serve as a treasure trove of genuine antiquities and repro trinkets. The former Dongtai Road antique street market fell victim to the developer's wrecking ball in 2015 and the entire street has since been wiped off the map to make way for luxury apartments and glitzy malls, like Hubindao (150 Hubin Road). Don't believe the signs posted around the area saying that the market has been transferred elsewhere – it hasn't.

Instead, vintage hunters should head to the multi-level **Cang Bao Lou Building** on the corner of Fangbang Road and Henan Road. It's known as the Ghost Market, because serious traders and collectors arrive in the ghostly hours before dawn. Although you don't need to be quite so zealous, this is definitely a morning destination – the good stuff is gone by early afternoon. Keep an eye out for antique furnishings and decorative pieces, rare books and other pre-1949 ephemera, including opium pipes, old maps and engraved cutlery.

Continuing toward Yu Gardens, the faux-traditional shophouses along Fangbang Road carry a variety of souvenir knick-knacks and Maomorabilia with humorous gift potential. Be sure to bargain hard since there is strong competition between vendors for their stash of bronze doorknockers, colourful Cultural Revolution statues and 1930s 'Shanghai Girl' advertising posters.

For a break between shopping, climb the rickety wooden staircase to the delightful **Old Shanghai Teahouse**. Decorated with old gramophones, cut glass mirrors and other genuine 1930s decor, this musty-magnificent tearoom serves pots of tea and soup noodles.

*Cang Bao Lou Building; 57 Fangbang Middle Road; daily 5am–5pm; map E4*
*Old Shanghai Teahouse; 385 Fangbang Middle Road; map E4*

# Get kitted out with a custom-made wardrobe at the South Bund fabric market

Sartorially speaking, it's difficult to beat the buzz of getting a suit or dress made and measured especially for you. While the benevolent charm of a professional tailor is sadly absent at South Bund, you can't beat this bustling market for sheer variety of fabric and absurdly low prices.

The market is located in the south of Shanghai's Old Town where you can meander through the traditional *longtang* (lane housing) that's been largely bulldozed in other parts of the city. Spread over three floors, the market is a hive of vendors. Most of the cost is the fabric (labour is cheap) so expect to pay more for quality threads. You can either copy something you already own, use a computer printout or draw your own design, though it's best to stick to classic cuts – think pencil skirt or pea coat. Most items take a week to make, but you can pay extra to expedite the process.

**Where to go and what to buy**

For a buttery-soft leather jacket, **stall 195** has a good range of tan, black and even bright leathers and will make a biker jacket for around RMB800. Dashing tuxedos can be found at **stall 137**, which does the lot – suit, shirt, tie and cummerbund – for RMB900 with a 24-hour express service. Classic suits (RMB700) are made well at **stall 326**, where some English is spoken. Just down the hall, Eric Chang at **stall 310** makes excellent fitted shirts for RMB85.

For casual wear, some of the best prices at the market are at **stall 285**, which offers a wide range of cotton and linen and is best at copying shorts (RMB100) or trousers (RMB170). Meanwhile, **stall 215** stocks reams of luscious cashmere from charcoal to camel. It's difficult to get them below RMB700 for a cashmere coat – a good sign as it means it's pure. Stunning silks can be found at **stall 136**, with block colours costing RMB45 per metre and tussah silk costing RMB75. Finally, for *qipaos* (Chinese dresses) **stall 186** has a good selection of styles and a competitive price at RMB350.

*South Bund Fabric Market; 399 Lujiabang Road; tel: 6377 7288; daily 9am–6pm; map G1*

# Share a special lunch at Table No. 1, then relax on a sun lounger at Sunny Beach

At midday, everything in Shanghai stops for lunch. From hole-in-the-wall kiosks to upscale eateries, lunch is a very big deal. One of Shanghai's most in-demand lunchtime spots is **Table No. 1** by Jason Atherton on the ground floor of The Waterhouse at the South Bund boutique hotel. Jason Atherton was the first British chef to complete a stint at Ferran Adrià's el Bulli in Spain, and his time at Gordon Ramsay's Maze in London saw it gain a Michelin star. Table No. 1 in Shanghai was Atherton's first solo project and sparked his swiftly expanding global gourmet empire. The spare but stylish dining room and courtyard terrace serves modern European cuisine with a focus on light seasonal dishes prepared for sharing. The lunch menu – which changes every two weeks – comprises tasting and tapas dishes cooked and presented in a modern style, such as roasted squid with almond puree, cucumber and olives, or sweetcorn and basil velouté with braised duck. A cocktail bar with fine evening river views and a herb garden crown the rooftop.

After lunch, it's time to head to the beach. The coastline near

Shanghai isn't suitable for swimming, so in 2011 the city created a man-made sandy beach for sun worshippers beside the Huangpu River. Close to The Waterhouse at South Bund, Sunny Beach has sun loungers, parasols – and views of the Pudong skyline. Weekend pool parties are occasionally held throughout the summer months.

*Waterhouse at South Bund, 1–2 Maojiayuan Road, nr Zhongshan Road South; tel: 6080 2999; www.tableno-1.com; map H3*

# Step aboard a cruise boat after dark and sail along the neon-lit Huangpu River

The Huangpu River is more than just Shanghai's visual centrepiece – it is the city's lifeblood. Connecting the East China Sea and the mighty Yangtze River, it facilitated the earliest fishing vessels whose owners formed Shanghai's original riverside settlement. Nineteenth-century development saw coastal junks and, later, barges, trans-continental merchant vessels and cruise liners ply the muddy waters, converting Shanghai into a city of globalised trade.

Shanghai's tidal economic artery pulses with an additional revenue source: tourism. Day and night river cruises are extremely popular with Chinese tourists. It's easy to see why, as the broad river offers a unique photographic vantage point contrasting Shanghai's east and west banks.

Several cruise operators (mostly offering a similar route and price point, and ranging in size from 80-seaters to a 1,000-person multi-deck cruiser) depart from the revamped Shiliupu wharf south of the Bund (in front of Hotel Indigo). The route heads north to view the Pudong skyline and international cruise terminal, then loops south along the Bund towards the city's impressive bridges and the 2010 Shanghai World Expo site. Some cruises take you further toward the mouth of the Yangtze River.

The most photogenic river trip is after dark, when the skyline of modern towers and heritage buildings is illuminated, and the cruise boats switch on their own bright neon bulbs. Evening cruises run each night between 6.30 and 9.30pm, departing at 30-minute intervals and taking approximately 45 minutes. Tickets (RMB100) can be bought at the terminal before boarding. The Peninsula Shanghai and Mandarin Oriental Pudong, Shanghai hotels also have their own luxury yachts available to charter for bespoke cruising.

*Shiliupu Wharf; Zhongshan No. 2 Road East; map G4*

# Get up close to the grand-scale engineering of the Lupu Bridge

Spanning the Huangpu River between Luwan and Pudong, the uber-impressive **Lupu Bridge** (built 2003) is the world's second-longest arch bridge, behind Chongqing's Chaotianmen (which pipped it by two metres in 2010). Its main span is 550 metres (1,804ft) and it rises 100 metres (328ft) above the river. Unique in design, it mixes cable-stay, arch and suspension technology, and is built to withstand a force-12 hurricane and an earthquake measuring 7 on the Richter scale.

Until a few years ago, it was possible to ascend the Lupu Bridge. Those willing to take on the 367 steps were rewarded with 360-degree views of Shanghai, from the 2010 World Expo site across to the ocean in the distance, and the dense forest of downtown skyscrapers. However, it is closed at time of writing; keep an eye out for changes in the future to this situation.

In the meantime, find a good vantage spot from which to admire this feat of engineering; it is impressive by day and possibly even more so lit up at night.

*Lupu Bridge; 909 Luban Road; off map D1*

# Spice up your life with piquant Yunnanese food and exotic cocktails

**Lost Heaven** is a four-storey Yunnanese restaurant that does a splendid job of putting the cuisine of this picturesque corner of China on the map. The exotic menu showcases 'Mountain Mekong' cuisine, a fusion of ingredients, spices and culinary preparations found along an ancient trading route that connected Yunnan with Burma and Thailand. The rich meat, seafood and vegetable dishes are flavoured with Thai spices, Burmese curry sauces and Yunnan's rich, meaty mountain mushrooms, which are widely used in soups and hot pots.

The interior is decorated in Dai, Bai and Miao ethnic minority style, with exotic facemasks and Buddhist statuettes, while staff wear traditional dress and pictures of Yunnan adorn the walls. Pre- or after-dinner cocktails can be enjoyed on the spacious rooftop bar terrace. Lost Heaven also has a smaller branch and lounge in the former French Concession.

*Lost Heaven; 17 Yan'an Road East; tel: 6330 0967; www.lostheaven.com.cn; map E5*
*Lost Heaven, French Concession; 38 Gaoyou Road; tel: 6433 5126; map page 88, B2*
*Southern Barbarian: 2/F, Ju'Roshine Life Arts Space, 169 Jinxian Road; tel: 5157 5510; www.southernbarbarian.com; map page 88, F5*

### Southern Barbarian

If Lost Heaven serves an exotic blend of style and spice, Southern Barbarian in the former French Concession specialises in homely Yunnan cooking in a more bohemian atmosphere. Its hearty barbecued meats, fried goat's cheese, fresh herbs and piquant broths can be washed down with a supreme selection of craft brews from the United States, Australia and Belgium.

# Splash out on a tailor-made party dress by one of Shanghai's best-known fashion designers

Many visitors to Shanghai head straight to their favourite local tailor for a new made-to-measure wardrobe. But for something extra special, why not make like a celebrity and have your own custom couture fitting?

Home-spun talent **Lu Kun** is an edgy couturier to local TV, movie and pop stars – and even Paris Hilton. Born in 1981, Lu studied fashion design at a local academy and took up an apprenticeship in a tailor's workshop on graduation. At the age of 22, Lu established his own studio and the following year won a trifecta of fashion accolades: the Shanghai Top Ten Designer Award, Nokia Fashion Diamond Award and the China Pioneer Designer of The Year, catapulting him into sartorial stardom.

Fittingly, Lu's style is very much rooted in his love for Shanghai, especially its jazzy 1930s era. His designs incorporate obvious Chinese elements and fabrics but with a bold, contemporary and very feminine flair. Exquisite tailoring remains at the forefront of his craft.

For ladies looking for a one-of-a-kind party dress or elegant evening wear, Lu conducts personal fittings by appointment only in his studio near Xintiandi. Pieces take

from a few days to several weeks depending on complexity, and the studio can arrange shipping of the finished piece if necessary. Alternatively, you can rifle through the racks of fashions in Lu's studio and have your chosen outfit specially adjusted on the spot.

*Lu Kun Studio; Room 520, 92 Huangjiaque Road; tel: 139 1699 6057; map D2*

# PEOPLE'S SQUARE AND JING AN

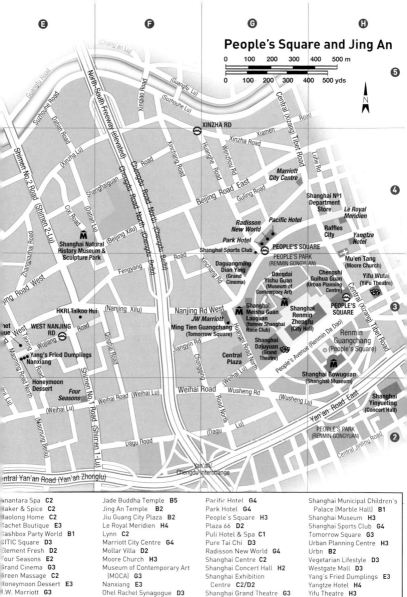

# People's Square and Jing An

| | | | |
|---|---|---|---|
| 0    100   200   300   400   500 m | | | |
| 0    100   200   300   400   500 yds | | | |

**E**    **F**    **G**    **H**

**5**

(Chang'an Lu)

Guangfu Road

(Chang'an Lu)

Suzhouhe Lu (Suzhouhe Lu)

Shimen No.2 Road (Shimen 2-Lu)

North-South Freeway (elevated)

Xinjiaqu Lu

(Guangfu Lu)

Datian Road

Chengdu Road North (Chengdu Beilu)

Shanghaiguan Road

Xinchang Road

Suzhouhe Lu

XINZHA RD

Xinzha Road

Xiamen Road

Huanghe Road

Wenzhou Road

Luhe Rd

Central (Xizang) Tibet Road

**4**

(Xinzha Lu)

Chi Road (Datian Lu)

Shanghai Natural History Museum & Sculpture Park

Beijing Road East

Guling Road

Marriott City Centre

Shanghai Nº1 Department Store

Le Royal Meridien

Zhongshan Road West

Fengyang Road

Nanjing (Nanjing Xilu)

Radisson New World

Pacific Hotel

Xinchang Road

Park Hotel

Shanghai Sports Club

PEOPLE'S SQUARE

Raffles City

Yangtze Hotel

Road

Daguangming Dian Ying (Grand Cinema)

Chengdu Road North (Chengdu Beilu)

PEOPLE'S PARK (RENMIN GONGYUAN)

Dangdai Yishu Guan (Museum of Contemporary Art)

Chengshi Guihua Guan (Urban Planning Centre)

Mu'en Tang (Moore Church)

Yifu Wutai (YiFu Theatre)

ing Road West

Qinghai Road

HKRI Taikoo Hui

Nanjing Rd West

(Nanjing Xilu)

JW Marriott

Shanghai Meishu Guan Laoguan (former Shanghai Race Club)

Shanghai Renmin Zhengfu (City Hall)

PEOPLE'S SQUARE

WEST NANJING RD

Wujiang Road

Ming Tien Guangchang (Tomorrow Square)

Huangpi Road West

Renmin Guangchang (People's Square)

net que West

Yang's Fried Dumplings Nanxiang

Jiangyin Rd

Central Plaza

Chongqing Road

Shanghai Dajuyuan (Grand Theatre)

People's Avenue (Renmin Da Dao)

Maoming Road North

Honeymoon Dessert

Four Seasons

Weihai Road (Weihai Lu)

Wusheng Rd

Road North

People's Avenue (Renmin Da Dao)

Shanghai Bowuguan (Shanghai Museum)

(Weihai Lu)

Weihai Road

(Wusheng Lu)

Shanghai Yinyueting (Concert Hall)

Maoming Belu

Dagu Road

(Dagu Lu)

Yan'an Road East

PEOPLE'S PARK (RENMIN GONGYUAN)

**2**

Shimen No.1 Road (Shimen 1-Lu)

entral Yan'an Road (Yan'an Zhonglu)

Yan'an/ Chengdu Interchange

Central Jinling Road

**E**    **F**    **G**    **H**

# Go museum-hopping around the oval-shaped People's Square

Shanghai's largest public space, People's Square, contains an impressive triumvirate of museums in the heart of downtown.

Founded in 2005 by Hong Kong jewellery trader Samuel Kung, the **Shanghai Museum of Contemporary Art** (MOCA) occupies a converted greenhouse in a corner of People's Park. The glassy, two-floor space is connected by a sloping walkway that overlooks the downstairs exhibitions. Although small, MOCA shows some of the more cutting-edge, thought-provoking art in the city from abstract Chinese and contemporary Indian to Pierre et Gilles erotic photography, Gaudi's architecture and Pixar animation.

Exit the park past the former Shanghai Race Club with its signature clocktower and SRC insignia above the entrance dating from 1933. Across the road is the **Grand Cinema**, host venue of the annual Shanghai International Film Festival. Also opened in 1933, the 2,000-seat cinema was the finest of its time in China with bold Art Deco lines and cubes across the facade, marble-panelled doors and lobbies shaped like cashew nuts.

It was renovated in 2008, adding a new sound system and seating, a rooftop bar and restaurant, and an intriguing History Walk. Follow the circular corridor, which tells the Grand's storied 80-year history through sepia photos, newspaper ads and movie clips. Most of the narration is in Chinese, but the historic images juxtaposing Hollywood glamour and Communist China are illuminating.

Shaped like a *ding*, an ancient Chinese cooking vessel, **Shanghai Museum** hold's China's finest collection of ancient arts and crafts. Designed by Chinese architect, Xing Tonghe (who also designed the Urban Planning Centre, see page 70), the massive five-storey granite structure opened in 1996. Allow at least a full morning for your visit, as this place is seriously large. The museum claims to have 120,000 exhibits. The 11 permanent galleries are themed according to a particular aspect of Chinese culture, ranging from jade carving, coins and ceramics to calligraphy, ethnic minority arts and bronze works. A hand-held audioguide is recommended for touring each section. Two temporary galleries host occasional painting exhibitions by Chinese and global artists. The extensive museum shop is one of the finest of its kind in China.

*MOCA; Gate 7, People's Park, 231 Nanjing Road West; tel: 6327 9900; www.mocashanghai.org; daily 10am–6pm; charge; map G3*
*Grand Cinema; 216 Nanjing Road West (entrance to the History Walk is at No. 248); tel: 6327 1899; www.shdgm.com (Chinese only); map G3*
*Shanghai Museum; People's Avenue; tel: 6327 5300; www.shanghaimuseum.net; daily 9am–5pm, last entrance at 4pm; free; map H3*

### Showcase Shanghai

The People's Square area is Shanghai's exact geographical midpoint. The main metro lines all converge here, transporting people from all over the city to its cultural and political hub. The core of People's Square today is Showcase Shanghai: world-class museums, a theatre, five-star hotels, and the imposing Shanghai City Hall in the middle of it all. The buildings, all raised in the 1990s and each one a significant architectural statement, symbolise Shanghai's arrival as a city that can compete on its own merit on the world stage.

# Scope out Shanghai's future landscape at the Urban Planning Exhibition Centre

Over the last three decades, Shanghai has been in a massive state of flux, and within this short period virtually the entire city has been relandscaped and reinvented. The Urban Planning Exhibition Centre helps to make some sense of the renovation and building frenzy that continues apace. Designed by Xing Tonghe, it occupies a whitewashed modern building with a strikingly uplifted roof – a contemporary twist on an ancient Chinese city gate. Inside the lobby is a gold-coloured installation entwining Shanghai's signature structures, which has become a popular photo-op spot.

From here, most visitors make a beeline for the third floor, with good reason. The centrepiece exhibit, viewed from an elevated walkway, is a vast scale model of Shanghai as it will look in 2020. You can peruse the entire cityscape, mentally checking off the signature buildings – including the 632-metre (2073ft) Shanghai Centre Tower, the city's loftiest supertower.

Don't neglect the other floors, however. The first floor is dedicated to Concession-era development, and features superb old photos of the construction of French- and European-style villas and streets. There's also a scale model of the Waibaidu Bridge.

The second floor focuses on Shanghai's contemporary urban construction, in particular the range of mega projects that have sprung up since the 1990s.

The fourth floor showcases transportation developments, notably the expansion of both city airports, the metro system and the ongoing rehabilitation of Suzhou Creek.

*Shanghai Urban Planning Exhibition Centre; 100 Renmin Avenue; tel: 6318 4477; www.supec.org; Tue–Sun 9.30am–5pm; charge; map H3*

# Enjoy a classical concert or ballet at one of Shanghai's world-class performance venues

People's Square is Shanghai's Culture Central. In addition to modern and classical art and the city's best museums, it houses two world-class performance venues, the Shanghai Grand Theatre and Shanghai Concert Hall.

In 2004, the stately **Shanghai Concert Hall** was awarded more than a makeover ahead of its 75th birthday. Plagued by the noise and pollution of the Yan'an Highway on its doorstep, it was decided that the concert hall should be moved. So the 5,650-tonne neoclassical building was hoisted 3.38 metres (11ft 1in) and slowly moved 66.46 metres (218ft) southeast on special rollers. The cost of shifting it out of harm's way was a cool RMB150 million.

Founded in 1930, as the Nanking Theatre, it opened with a performance of the hit musical *Broadway*. Over the years, Chinese opera star Mei Lanfang, pianist Lang Lang and cellist Yoyo Ma, among other great musicians, have all performed here. Enlarged to host 1,200 concertgoers, it is now considered one of Asia's premier classical concert venues, attracting symphony orchestras and performers from around the world.

Contrasting with the Concert Hall's classical facade, the **Shang-hai Grand Theatre**, designed by lauded French architect Jean-Marie Charpentier, is a futuristic glass confection with flamboyantly upturned eaves – mimicking a traditional Chinese roof – that glow magically at night when the interior lights come on. A varied programme ranges from stellar classical concerts to ballet and theatre. Among the performers to have graced the stage are Sir Simon Rattle and the Berlin Philharmonic orchestra, Japanese violin virtuoso Midori, and Ballet Preljocaj.

*Shanghai Grand Theatre; 300 Renmin Avenue; tel: 6327 6740; www.shgtheatre. com; map G3*
*Shanghai Concert Hall; 523 Yan'an East Road; tel: 5386 6666; www.shanghai concerthall.org; map H2*

# Take a stroll through a Sculpture Park and discover dinosaur bones at the Shanghai Natural History Museum

Established in 1956, the Shanghai Natural History Museum was gifted a new architectural landmark in the downtown Jing'An Sculpture Park in 2015, with the capacity to display its 10,000-plus pieces across a whopping 45,000sqm. Designed by Perkins+Will and inspired by a nautilus shell, the six-story building with a spiralling grass-topped roof, coils around a central canyon of Chinese-style landscaped rockeries and waterfalls, filling the underground exhibition spaces with natural light. Starting on the top floor, visitors descend through a series of beautifully designed spaces describing various aspects of creation and evolution, accompanied by bilingual background notes on touchscreens. Fossils and bones are brought to life through a menagerie of full-size moving models of ancient mammoths, whales and other wildlife. Fun interactive technology includes machines to measure the cranial capacity of human skulls and 360-degree movie pods. But it's the Chinese dinosaur skeletons that steal the show, including a Tyrannosaurus whose roar echoes through the museum galleries. The journey winds up at the base of the central atrium where recreated skeletons of Asia's largest dinosaurs, including the 26-metre-long Mamenchisaurus, a 140-million-year-old dinosaur from China, provide a last jaw-gaping impression and spectacular photo ops against the Chinese garden backdrop.

The museum is set within a manicured park that is well worth a stroll on a pleasant day to check out large-scale sculptures, blooming peach blossoms in spring and the occasional calligraphy master practicing Chinese characters in water on the flagged stones.

*Shanghai Natural History Museum; 128 Shimen No. 2 Road; tel: 5228 9562; Tue–Sun 9am–3.30pm; map E3*

# Take an architectural tour of the city centre's landmark hotels

Ever since the 1920s, hotel architecture has influenced the development of the Shanghai skyline. People's Square boasts a number of landmark hotel buildings worth a closer look.

When the eight-storey **Pacific Hotel** (108 Nanjing Road West; map G4) went up in 1924, it was the tallest building in Shanghai. A blend of neoclassical, baroque and Art Deco styles, its best features are the façade balconies and crowning cupola.

Completed soon after in 1926, the Yangtze Hotel (740 Hangkou Road; map H4) is an eight-level Art Deco monument, with bold symmetrical lines and motifs. Reopened in 2009, the interior boasts a stylishly updated 1920s decor.

Next, in 1928, came the 10-storey **Shanghai Sports Club** (150 Nanjing Road West; map G3) with its mosaic brick facade and twin Art Deco towers. The front section is now the Bank of Shanghai, and a sports club occupies the upper levels.

When it opened in 1934, the 24-storey **Park Hotel** (170 Nanjing Road West; map G4) was Asia's tallest building. Clad in dark Taishan brick, the pioneering luxury Art Deco hotel once featured a rooftop nightclub overlooking the Shanghai

racecourse. Sepia-tinted photos of those halcyon days hang around the second-floor history gallery.

Today, these wonders of Old Shanghai stand in the shadows of several modern high-rise structures. Soaring over the landscape is the 60-floor Tomorrow Square tower, home to the **JW Marriott Shanghai** (399 Nanjing Road West; map G3). This glassy, space-age structure twists on its own axis then slims into a hollow pinnacle reaching toward the sky. At its apex is the world's highest library.

# Lay back and enjoy a green tea or Traditional Chinese Medicine (TCM) spa treatment

The Jing An CBD typifies Shanghai's increasingly in vogue work-hard, play-hard lifestyle. But when you need to escape the crowds and noise of the metropolis, there are plenty of spas and massage venues offering unique, relaxing treatments.

In the sexy Puli Resort & Spa, **Anantara**'s treatment menu, inspired by the healing power of Chinese tea, offers green tea wraps, white tea scrubs and rose tea beautification packages, plus some of the best massages in Shanghai.

On the upstairs level of the Shanghai Centre, **Green Mas-sage** is a long-time favourite for well-priced Chinese massages in elegant surrounds. Try the rousing traditional Chinese acupressure massage or foot reflexology. Or go for something a little more left-field, like the aromatic ear candling treatment.

Another local favourite for well-priced spa and massage treatments is **Dragonfly**. The contemporary urban retreat has a romantic Southeast Asian ambience and offers a menu of sports and oil massages plus Biodroga facials, nail services and waxing. There are several Dragonfly locations around the city including a convenient branch in the basement of Jing An Kerry Centre. A welcome stop for a soothing foot massage after walking along lengthy Nanjing Road.

*Anantara Spa; 3/F, 1 Changde Road; tel: 2216 6899; spa.anantara.com/shanghai; map C2*
*Green Massage; 202 West Retail Plaza, Shanghai Centre, 1376 Nanjing Road West; tel: 6289 7776; www.greenmassage.com.cn; map C2*
*Dragonfly; Shop #25, SB1-05B, B/1 South Retail, Jing An Kerry Centre, 1218 Yan'an Middle Road; tel: 6266 0018; www.dragonfly.net.cn; map C2*

# Sample a variety of plump Shanghai dumplings on Wujiang Road

During the 1920s, Wujiang Road was known as Love Lane and was lined with bordellos and ballrooms. In later decades, the east end of the road became a popular street food market of curbside griddles and ramshackle restaurants. Today, the redeveloped Wujiang Road Pedestrian Street is home to international high street brands including Marks & Spencer, Baskin-Robbins and Starbucks.

Happily for fans of Shanghai dumplings, one of the food street's original dumpling purveyors survived and upgraded to a small store on the second floor of Infiniti Mall. **Yang's Fried Dumplings** remains a local institution on account of one thing: *shengjian*. These doughy Shanghai dumplings are filled with tender pork and rich broth, sprinkled with sesame seeds and chopped chives, and fried in a griddle till their bottoms are toasty golden. Remember to pay first (RMB5 per four dumplings), then join the queue as you watch the buns fry in large shallow pans.

On the same floor, you can also find **Nanxiang**, another famous Shanghai dumpling restaurant with a popular branch in Yu Garden. Nanxiang is best known for its *xiaolongbao*. These pork and crabmeat steamed dumplings, also native to Shanghai, are shaped like little money pouches. The delicate skins barely manage to contain the juicy meat and soup, which explodes deliciously in your mouth.

*Yang's Fried Dumplings; 2/F, Infiniti Mall, 269 Wujiang Road; tel: 6136 1391*
*Nanxiang; 2/F, Infiniti Mall, 269 Wujiang Road; tel: 6136 1428; map E3*

### How to eat a dumpling

Both varieties of soup dumpling can be a mouth-burning hazard for the uninitiated. The trick is to bite a small hole at the top to allow the steam to escape. Then carefully suck out the soup, dip in black vinegar and devour in a single bite before all that greasy goodness dribbles down your chin.

# Limber up with tai chi at Jing An Park or light an incense stick at Jing An Temple

The area around **Jing An Temple** was formerly called Bubbling Well Road on account of a natural spring that once bubbled to the surface. A temple has existed on this revered site since 1216. For anyone passing Jing An Temple today, sandwiched between luxury shopping malls and a busy intersection, it's clear that the large gold-capped Buddhist temple is not an ancient construct. In fact, it is in a constant state of development as the wealthy abbot continues to add grandiose embellishments. Latest additions include a 63-metre (207ft) lotus-shaped gilded pagoda and a five-storey Precious Hall of the Great Hero made of Burmese teak.

The abundance of ostentatious gold may seem at odds with Zen worship, but this Mi Buddhist sect has always been known for its wealthy tastes. Jing An Temple was the richest Buddhist temple in China prior to closure in 1949, when its abbot was famed for having seven mistresses and a White Russian bodyguard.

Perhaps not surprisingly, the temple is hugely popular in prosperity-hungry Shanghai. Locals pack the grounds praying for luck and fortune, especially at Chinese New Year, when the monks charge hundreds of yuan for entrance. For the tourist, the most impressive view is from outside, as the interiors of the temple suffered heavily during the Cultural Revolution when it was used as a plastics factory.

A much more Zen-like retreat is **Jing An Park**, opposite the

temple. This small urban park filled with shady groves, lily ponds and walk-through rockeries is a hive of activity throughout the day. From the large crowds of elderly tai chi enthusiasts engaged in early morning shadow boxing, to the groups of men huddled over games of Chinese chess, and the couples that come to ballroom dance in the early evening, there's always plenty of activity. The Chinese garden (RMB2 entrance) has a lovely little alfresco teahouse perfect for peaceful contemplation.

*Jing An Temple; 1686 Nanjing Road West; daily 7am–5pm; RMB10; map B2*
*Jing An Park; 1649 Nanjing Road West; daily 5am–6pm; free; map B1*

# Belt it like a rock star during a late-night karaoke session

Living out your rock star fantasies has become a popular pastime around the world, but nowhere has quite so many dedicated closet crooners as karaoke-crazed China. Karaoke – pronounced *ka-la-OK* – rates above bars and clubs as the most popular form of evening entertainment in a culture where alcohol-fuelled socialising is traditionally accompanied by drinking games and other diversions.

Of course, karaoke is not confined to evening hours. Business delegations frequently break out the microphones as a way of relaxing mid-meeting (many hotels have fully-equipped karaoke rooms as part of their conference centres). It's a well-known fact of corporate etiquette that business travellers should have a rehearsed version of *My Way* up their sleeves when being entertained by Chinese clients.

The most popular KTV parlours are generally grandiose affairs with scores of private rooms that operate around the clock. **Cashbox Party World** is the most popular chain, with several outlets across town. Private singing suites, accommodating up to 30 people, are equipped with a large-screen TV and high-tech audio equipment. An extensive compilation of songs is available in both Chinese and English. There's also a full drinks and snacks menu delivered by uniformed staff – it's common for groups to order several bottles of hard liquor to lubricate their vocal cords.

Rooms can be booked in one-hour or all-night blocks and prices vary depending on the time, with daytime and after midnight offering better deals. Be sure to book ahead during peak hours.

*Cashbox Party World; 109 Yandang Road; tel: 6374 1111; www.cashbox.com.tw; map B1*

# Hunt out the best cafés for your morning caffeine fix

Tea may be China's traditional beverage, but upwardly mobile Shanghainese are fast cultivating a taste for java. Global franchise coffee chains continue to percolate across the city, with adapted menus for local tastes (green tea or red bean frappucino, anyone?). These are joined by more charming local coffee shops, many offering free Wi-Fi with your brew.

For your morning java jump-start in Jing An, follow the scent of roasting beans and hot cinnamon to **Baker & Spice** at the Shanghai Centre, a massive complex of serviced residences, restaurants and a Ritz-Carlton hotel. Managed by Shanghai-based expats (who also own the popular café chain, Wagas), Baker & Spice is a tempting bakery café that brews a decent 'long black' or 'flat white' along with delicious pastries, mueslis and quiches from the glass display cases. The large, sunlit space with communal rustic wooden benches and a wraparound balcony overlooking Nanjing Road is a great place to watch white-collar Shanghai kick-start its day. Tiny **Sumerian** café brews some of the city's best coffee, including a cold-brew nitro coffee that looks like Guinness. They also serve hand-rolled American bagels,

cookies and delicious soft-serve yogurt. The popular café spills out onto the pavement during summer, with the two resident pooches adding to the fun.

Local chain **Seesaw** has also gained a reputation for its excellent coffee and barista academy. Try its fine brews at the sunny flagship in the atrium of a boutique office on Yuyuan Road, or at its growing number of refueling points across town.

*Baker & Spice; 1/F, 1376 Nanjing Road West; tel: 6289 8875; map C2*
*Sumerian; 415 Shaanxi North Road; tel: 138 1839 0441; map D3*
*Seesaw; Room 101, 433 Yuyuan Road; tel: 137 6170 0535; www.seesawcoffee.com; map A1*

# Shop 'til you drop along Nanjing Road West and stop for a reviving tea or tipple

The east end of Shanghai's major east–west commercial thoroughfare was historically Shanghai's premier shopping zone (see page 45). Nowadays, the high-end brand shopping has migrated to Nanjing Road West, with glassy shopping malls lining the stretch between Shimen Road and Jing An Temple.

Starting near Jing An Temple, **Reel Mall** (1601 Nanjing Road West; map B2) above Jing An Temple metro station (Line 2 and 7) houses fashionable restaurants and a good food hall in the basement. Opposite, the massive **Jing An Kerry Centre** (1515 Nanjing West Road; map C2) is chock-full of international fashion brands, cafés and restaurants, plus a cinema and Shangri-La hotel.

**Shanghai Centre** (1376 Nanjing Road West; map C2) is another great stop-off point for lunch, with a handful of upscale cafés and restaurants

spanning everything from Din Tai Fung, French café Angelina and Alan Wong's to gourmet burger joints and bakeries. There's also an English-speaking pharmacy, a medical clinic and a basement supermarket stocked with imported foodstuffs.

The line of tinted-windowed, chauffeured limos outside **Plaza 66** (1266 Nanjing Road West; map D2) suggests its deep-pocketed Chinese clientele. Five marble-clad levels contain the likes of Louis Vuitton, Dior, Chanel and Cartier, where the impeccably groomed shop to the strains of live music in the atrium.

The top floor offers branches of popular local restaurants including Zen (great dim sum) and Pin Chuan (modern Sichuan). Seductive subterranean lounge Archie's beneath the Alfred Dunhill boutique is an ambient spot for a stiff drink or Cuban *puro* cigar between purchases.

**Westgate Mall** (1038 Nanjing Road; map D3) features a clutch of luxury brands and an Isetan department store with a small Chinese food court in the basement. Between the malls are more moderately priced fashion outlets, such as Zara, H&M, Uniqlo and Marks & Spencer.

Nanjing Road's latest deluxe addition, **HKRI Taikoo Hu**, is opening in 2017 on the corner of Shimen Road.

# See a quintessential Chinese Opera at the Yifu Theatre

Multi-coloured and beautifully tailored costumes, elaborate face-painting, high-pitched singing, traditional instruments, super-swift mask changes, slapstick humour and gentle social commentary are among the elements that have made Chinese opera enduringly popular. It is a highly demanding art: actors, who begin training as children, must learn to sing and dance, acquire an extensive repertoire of highly stylised gestures and perform acrobatics.

The best place to see a Chinese opera is in the round-fronted heritage building on Fuzhou Road, officially known as the Tianchan Peking Opera Centre Yifu Theatre. It first opened in 1925 as the Tianchan Theatre – at a time when Peking Opera was burgeoning as a popular form of visual and musical entertainment. Reconstructed in the early 1990s, it is now known locally as the **Yifu Theatre**.

A prestigious location for performers of Peking and other genres of traditional Chinese opera, the 928-seat Yifu Theatre (there are also nine private boxes) is home to the Shanghai Peking Opera Company, whose repertoire includes the popular *Legend of the White Snake*,

*Dream of Red Mansions* and *The Bride of Jiao Zhongqing*.

The Yifu Theatre also attracts leading Chinese operatic touring troupes from Beijing and across China, plus Taiwan and Hong Kong. There are performances most evenings, plus some matinee shows. Some shows offer English surtitles on digital screens. But even if you can't follow the dialogue and lyrics, watching a Peking opera represents a quintessential – and extremely colourful – Chinese cultural experience.

*Yifu Theatre; 701 Fuzhou Road; tel: 6322 5294; www.tianchan.com; map H3*

# Visit the marble mansion of a corporate titan, now an arts school for gifted children

Hemmed in by high-rises and high-ways in the middle of the Jing An commercial district, stately **Marble Hall** was the home of one of Shanghai's wealthiest Jewish families, the Kadoories. Sir Elly Kadoorie made his fortune in real estate and utilities, and established the Hong Kong and Shanghai Hotels group in 1866, which owns The Peninsula hotel brand. Built between 1918 and 1924, the stately whitewashed mansion was made from imported Italian stone. Legend has it that Sir Elly never intended it to be quite so ostentatious, but his British architect got carried away while the family was overseas. The long facade features columns, French windows and wide balconies. The interiors are even more opulent, with elaborate plasterwork, ornate fireplaces, a two-storey ballroom with marble walls and floors, and sweeping dual staircases.

Marble Hall is now home to the Children's Palace, an extra-curricular school for talented local children. Wander in during afternoon or weekend class times for a closer look.

*Marble Hall; 64 Yan'an Road West; tel: 6248 1850; daily 8.30am–8pm; free – not officially open to the public, so enquire via your concierge; map B1*

## Moller Villa

A little further along Yan'an Road, at the junction of Shaanxi Road, is another eye-catching historic homestead. **Moller Villa** (30 Shaanxi South Road; www.mollervilla.com; map D1) was the home of shipping magnate Eric Moller. The Disney-esque design, topped with turrets and gables, was supposedly inspired by his daughter's dream of a fairytale castle. The home is now a state-run guesthouse and you can enter to explore the pretty grounds and interiors of carved Swedish wood brought to Shanghai on Moller's ships.

# Pay your respects to two exquisite Jade Buddhas and bask in the tranquillity of the temple

The beautiful ochre-yellow Jade Buddha Temple in the northern Jing An suburbs is a great place to escape the crowds and experience some Zen Buddhist tranquillity. The temple was established in 1882 to house a collection of statues that were given to a Qing Dynasty Chinese abbot during his travels in Myanmar. The monk, Hui Gen, brought two of the most impressive back to Shanghai. A temple was built to house them, on land donated by a Qing official from a devoutly Buddhist family.

The temple is filled with a number of beautifully carved statues. However, the stars of the show are the two jade Buddhas, each one carved from a single piece of jade. The larger is the seated Buddha, measuring 1.95 metres (6.5ft) and weighing in at three tonnes. The creamy white, almost luminous statue shows Buddha at the moment of enlight-enment. The smaller (96cm/37in), but more exquisite reclining Jade Buddha, depicts a tranquil Buddha at the moment of death.

The jade Buddhas are displayed in a special hall at the north end of the temple. The rest of the temple includes the Hall of the Heavenly Kings with a big image of the laughing Buddha, and The Grand Hall with the image of the Buddha meditating on a lotus leaf, flanked by the warri-or-like gods of the 20 heavens.

The restaurant on the eastern side of the temple serves vegetarian noodles for RMB5 a dish downstairs, and more elaborate meals on the second floor. Shops in the streets around the temple sell Buddhist paraphernalia like prayer beads and portraits.

*Jade Buddha Temple; 170 Anyuan Road; tel: 6266 3668; daily 8am–4.30pm; charge; map B5*

# Join local monks for a Chinese vegetarian feast

If you spot a monk in a saffron robe scurrying past a Nanjing Road luxury brand mall, don't assume he has struck gold and is seeking a watch or designer bag. Rather than shopping, he is most likely heading for dinner at **Vegetarian Lifestyle**.

Meaty flavours and a predilection for exotic ingredients render much of China's cuisine off-limits for vegetarians. But this welcoming, modern Chinese vegetarian restaurant, just one block back from downtown Nanjing Road West, caters especially for meat-free mavens. It is also egg-free and MSG-free, and serves no alcohol. The varied Chinese fare – plus neat presentation and efficient service – packs in the punters for lunch and dinner.

Vegetarian Lifestyle specialises in replica meat dishes, fashioned from tofu and gluten, plus a large menu of vegetable, noodle and rice dishes. The flavours of China are well represented, ranging from veggie versions of spicy Sichuan Mapo Doufu and Shanghainese fried dumplings to Yunnan-style salted beans and Hunanese peppered chicken. The freshly squeezed fruit juices come in a range of exotic flavours, while endless hot green tea is served free to all diners.

The restaurant is particularly busy on weekday lunchtimes, when office workers chow down on the excellent value RMB20 set lunch tray, featuring a selection of dishes of the day, plus rice and fruit. Unlike the picture-book main menu, the lunch specials are written only in Chinese characters – so just scan the room for someone cradling a blonde wood tray and point. The server will understand instantly.

For more recommendations and information on meat-free dining, contact the **Shanghai Vegetarians Club** at http://shanghaiveggie. webs.com.

*Vegetarian Lifestyle; 258 Fenxian Road; tel: 6215 7566; daily 11am–9pm; map D3*

# Learn the secrets of *taijijuan* from an English-speaking master at Pure Tai Chi

Pass any Shanghai park in the early morning hours or late in the afternoon and you'll spot elderly Shanghainese engaged in the slow, focused practice of *taijijuan* (known in English as tai chi). One look at their calm demeanors and surprising flexibility and it's easy to understand the benefits of this traditional form of exercise.

Rooted in the Chinese belief that good health is dependent on the smooth flow of energy *(qi)* around the body, *taijijuan* can be practised on many levels, from a simple 'meditative' system of hand poses to a powerful martial art.

Although the movements themselves don't seem physically challenging, the language barrier can make it difficult to grasp the minute details of each hand position, correct body placement and focus, coordination with breathing and understanding of the guiding philosophies.

**Pure Tai Chi** offers daily classes with master teachers – including national champions and professors – all of whom can communicate the intricacies of their art form in English. Students can choose from a range of styles – the contrasting Chen style and easier Yang version are the most popular, but there are also specialised combative varieties like Eight Section Brocade and 24 Style (not related to Jack Bauer). Due to the nature of tai chi, classes are generally conducted on a one-on-one basis. If you've time, this is a more beneficial way to learn than as part of a group.

Many luxury hotels also offer guided morning tai chi sessions – a great way to calm your mind, and develop coordination and focus for the day ahead.

*Pure Tai Chi; No. 201, Building 12, 470 Shaanxi Road North; tel: 5010 6707; www.puretaichi.com/en; map D3*

# FORMER FRENCH CONCESSION

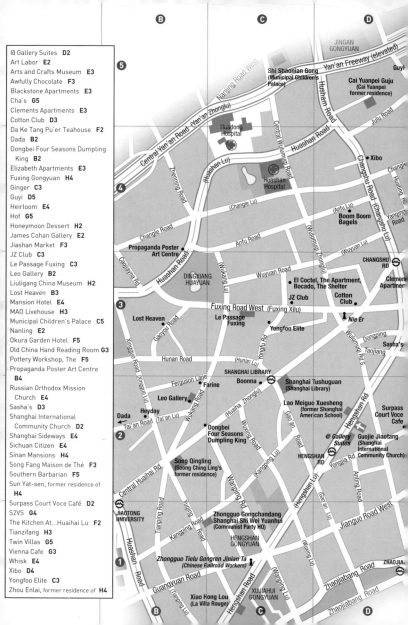

# French Concession

Southern Barbarian
Jinxian Road (Jinxian Lu)
Lanxin Daxiyuan (Lyceum Theatre)
(Julu Lu)
(Change Lu)
Change Road
Xiangyang Road North (Xiangyang Beilu)
Shaanxi Road South
Maoming Road South
Ruijin No.2 Road
Central Huaihai Road
Xing'an Rd
Isetan
Yandang Road
Chengdu Road South (Chengdu Nanlu)

The Pottery Workshop
Okura Garden Hotel
Guotai Dianyingyuan (Cathay Cinema)
New Hualian Commercial Building
Hof
Cha's
Nanchang Road
Yandang Entertainment Street
Chengdu Road South (Chengdu Nanlu)

Heirloom
Baisheng Gouwu Zhongxin (Parkson Department Store)
Twin Villas
S2VS
Sheng Nigulasi Jiaotang (former St Nicholas Church)

Liang
Mansion Hotel
Shanghai Sideways
Xinle
Xiangyang Gongyuan
Russian Orthodox Mission Church
(Huaihai)
SOUTH SHAANXI RD
Sichuan Citizen
Zhongguo Lanyin Huabu Guan (Chinese Printed Blue Nankeen Exhibition Hall)
Mansion Complex
Donghu Road
Nanchang Road
Gaolan Road
Sinan Road
FUXING GONGYUAN
Xiangshan Road
Sun Zhongshan Guju (former residence of Sun Yat-sen)
Central Fuxing Road
Sinan Mansions
Zhou Enlai Guju (former residence of Zhou Enlai)
Hotel Massenet
North-South Freeway (elevated)
Hefei Rd

Whisk
Central Huaihai Road
Yinyue Xueyuan (Conservatory of Music)
SOUTH SHAANXI RD
Xiangyang Road South
Nanchang Road
(Fuxing Zhonglu)

Elizabeth Apartments
Blackstone Apartments
Central Fuxing Road
Yongkang Road Bar Street
Yongkang Road
Wenhua Guangchang (Cultural Square)
Ruijin No.2 Road
Yongjia Road
Ruijin Yi Yuan (Ruijin Hospital)
MAO Livehouse
Sinan Rd

Pushkin Triangle
Fenyang Rd
Shanghai Gongyi Meishuguan (Arts and Crafts Museum)
Puxijin (Pushkin)
Shaanxi Road South
Song Fang Maison de Thé
Shaoxing Road (Shaoxing Lu)
Vienna Café
Old China Hand Reading Room
Central Jianguo Road
Jiande Road

Art Labor
Taiyuan Road
Yongjia Lu
Damuqiao Road
Jiashan Market
Jianguo Road West
Ruijin 2-Lu
Taikang Road
Hay, Platane
Tianzifang
Ziao San Tang
Museum Café
Casa Pagoda
Liuligang China Museum

Nanling Rd
Yueyang Rd
Damuqiao Lu
Da Ke Tang Pu'er Teahouse
The Kitchen At...Huaihai Lu
Xiangyang Nanlu
DAPUQIAO
Honeymoon Dessert
Xujiahui Road
Xujiahui Lu

James Cohan Gallery
Taiyuan Road
Jianguo Xilu
Shaanxi Nanlu
Zhaojiabang Road
Zhaojiabang Road
JIASHAN RD

(Zhaojiabang Lu)
(Zhaojiabang Lu)

N

0    100   200   300   400   500 m
0    100   200   300   400   500 yds

E     F     G     H

# Meander the elegant streets of the French Concession, and admire architectural gems

Shanghai's soul resides within the charming tree-lined streets of the former French Concession. A stroll along its leafy boulevards and hidden lanes evokes a less frenetic era before China began its ascent into superpowerdom.

Start on Xinle Road at the **Russian Orthodox Mission Church**. Built in 1934 for the Russian community that had fled the revolution, the sapphire-hued onion domes sit opposite a stone-fronted 1930s mansion once owned by an opium-dealing gangster, and which is now the **Mansion Hotel**. Hot foot it south along Xiangyang Road to Huaihai Road, home to the sleek IAPM mall, then cross over and head down Fenyang Road until you reach **Fuxing Road** which, with its vintage villas and canopy of lovely plane trees, is a classic French Concession street. Turn right and stroll over to admire the trio of fine Concession-era residences on the left – the French-style Clements Apartments (No. 1300), the darkly Gothic Blackstone Apartments (No. 1331) featuring two exquisite rounded stone balconies, and the Art Deco Elizabeth Apartments (No. 1327). Now double back to Fenyang Road and turn right. At No. 79 is the **Arts and Crafts Museum** (see page 103), a Renaissance-style gem and one of the few French villas open to the public.

Continue along Fenyang Road and through the tiny triangular park featuring a bronze bust of Pushkin donated in 1937 by Shanghai's Russian community. Up ahead is the charming **Dongping Road**, where three grand villas (Nos 7, 9 and 11) were built by the influential Soong family. On the corner with Hengshan Road (No. 11) is a striking painted mansion that belonged to TV Soong, the Kuomintang's finance minister. Built in 1920, this fabled abode is now **Sasha's** cosy first floor bar and beer garden, with an elegant second floor restaurant.

*French Concession walk: map E4–D3*

# Enter a world of French charm and Chinois chic at Yongfoo Elite

Yongfu Road, a quintessential French Concession street lined with photogenic villas and plane tree canopies, is far from Shanghai's madding crowd. In spite, or perhaps because of this soulful ambience, it has morphed into a sophisticated nightlife zone. The catalyst was **Yongfoo Elite**, an esoteric Chinois club/restaurant created by a retired Chinese fashion designer in the restyled former British Consulate.

Beyond the gated driveway and tree-filled garden, the villa's dining room, terrace and lounges are an artistic tapestry of antiques, mahoqany furnishings, vintage Gucci sofas, Art Deco lamps and ancient calligraphy works. There's even a 1930s opium bed in the garden. The dining room serves traditional Chinese dishes, alongside other menu selections infused with pan-Asian influences.

The pick of the three outhouse bars is Mission Lounge, where you can kick back on a leather sofa with a single malt and be transported back almost a century in time.

*Yongfoo Elite; 200 Yongfu Road; tel: 5466 2727; www.yongfooelite.com; 11am–midnight; map C3*

## Yongfu Road nightlife

Yongfu Road's alternative party palaces include **The Apartment** (3/F, 47 Yongfu Road; tel: 6437 9478; www.theapartment-shanghai.com), a casual loft-style cocktail lounge that transforms into a late-night dance club, with a spacious rooftop terrace. The second floor of the same building has a Spanish accent: **Bocado** (2/F, 47 Yongfu Road; 180 1727 0340) is a lively Spanish tapas restaurant and wine lounge, while Spanish chef Willy Trullas Moreno serves tapas and well-mixed cocktails at suave lounge, **El Coctel** (2/F, 47 Yongfu Road; tel: 6433 6511; www.el-coctel.com). The same chef owns a tiny hotdog stand at street-level below called **Bikini** (6433 6511) – for when the late-night munchies hit. Adding a little grunge to the street, live music venue The Shelter (B/F, 5 Yongfu Road) hosts independent electronic artists, DJs and new international alternative dance acts in a former bomb shelter.

# Shop for eco fashions, fun souvenirs and much more in the bustling alleys of Taikang Road

One of Shanghai's favourite souvenir hunting grounds is known as **Tianzifang** (map H3). Its labyrinthine alleys, filled with boutiques in former *shikumen* (stone-gated) homes, offer an atmospheric, if frenetic, alternative to the mega malls and high-end boutiques elsewhere. Over 100 shops, restaurants and street food stands occupy an ever-expanding network of alleys. Try to avoid visiting on weekends and holidays when it gets jam-packed.

Enter under the arched gate at 210 Taikang Road. One of the first studios you'll come to is that of **Deke Erh**. The Shanghainese photohistorian was a Tianzifang pioneer and his large warehouse showcases a collection of black and white prints charting the development of the city. Other boutiques can be found inside the **International Artists Factory** (Bldg 3, Lane 210 Taikang Road).

In the first courtyard to the left, **Kommune Café** is a favourite spot for sunny barbecue brunches. Deeper into the alleys, **Urban Tribe** (No. 14, Lane 248 Taikang Road; www.urbantribe.cn) is a top spot for items sourced from the owners' travels across remote western China.

There are plenty of local snacks to try in the lanes, from homemade yogurt to cumin-spiced barbecued kebabs. A good eat-in option is **East Eatery** (No 39, 155 Jianguo Middle Road; tel: 6467 0100; www.east-eatery.com), serving up a modern spin on Asian favourites.

Back on Taikang Road resides a trio of Shanghai's smartest home design stores. **Platane** (156 Taikang Road; www.platane.cn) showcases a beautifully edited contemporary lifestyle items, mostly hand-crafted in China. Danish design showroom **HAY** (176 Taikang Road; www.hay.dk) stocks functional pieces for fabulous homes, while **Casa Pagoda** (13–17 Taikang Road; www.casapagoda.com) is an eclectic emporium with glamorous home accessories.

You can't miss the huge stainless steel peony across the facade of the **Liuligang China Museum** (25 Taikang Road; www.liulichinamuseum.com), focussing on production of the colourful crystal ornaments.

# Take a ceremonial tea break at one of Shanghai's finest teahouses

The brewing, serving and drinking of tea remains a cherished ritual in China and every homestead has a stock of their favourite fresh leaves, be it green, oolong, black, white, pu'erh or flower tea. A traditional tea ceremony involves a meticulous process of heating the implements, washing the leaves and inhaling the scent, before sipping the infusion from thimble-like cups. After watching the ceremony, sit back and ruminate on life – with a pot of tea and snacks.

The elite **Da Ke Tang Pu'er Teahouse**, set in a handsome 1930s villa, specialises in premium pu'erh, a fermented compressed variety from Yunnan known as the 'Bordeaux of tea' on account of its dark ruby colour and expensive vintages. Enjoy the old Shanghai setting, free Wi-fi and snacks, but be prepared – fine tea comes at a price: in this case RMB300 is the minimum spend.

For a more contemporary interpretation, **Song Fang Maison de Thé** sells quality Chinese teas – from Fujianese oolong to Yunnanese varieties – and aromatic European blends. Leaves are packaged in *très*-chic aqua tins emblazoned with Chinese propaganda-style images that make great gifts. Sip your chosen brew in the cute upstairs tearoom.

If you only have time for a quick dip into Chinese tea culture, most streetside teashops will be happy to conduct a short tea ceremony for you to taste the different brews.

*Da Ke Tang Pu'er Teahouse; Lane 388 Xiangyang Road South; map F2*
*Song Fang Maison de Thé; 227 Yongjia Road; map F2*

# Shop for the latest fashions and accessories by Shanghai's promising young designers

Once considered the garment factory of the world, Chinese designers are finally gaining a global reputation for 'Created in China' style. Local boutique **Dong Liang** has a sharp eye for emerging Chinese fashion labels and indie designers and is the place to go to scope out the cutting edge of Chinese fashion talent. The multi-brand concept store has two standalone boutiques and an outlet shop in Shanghai – all within strolling distance of each other. Its newest store is the most beautiful yet (No. 2, Lane 764 Changle Road; tel: 6428 5320; en.

dongliangchina.com; map D4). The converted heritage terrace house features five inventively themed galleries, each showcasing a different Chinese designer, including Uma Wang, Boundless and Nicole Zhang. Enjoy an excellent barista brew in the sunny ground-floor cafe while browsing hip accessories and indie magazines. **The Crow House by Dong Liang** (Bldg 1, 888 Changle Road; tel: 6215 7855; map D4) is a small outlet beneath the company office selling out-of-season pieces at slightly discounted prices.

Stylish hommes should check out the young Shanghai-New York label, **S2VS** (172 Nanchang Road; map G4). Indonesian-born Sean William Salim creates preppy New York-style looks with sharp tailoring and fine attention to detail. His wallet-friendly designs are being snapped up by boutiques around the globe, but his tiny flagship boutique can be found in the front garden of a French Concession villa right here in Shanghai.

For handbag hounds, local label **Heirloom** (78 Xinle Road; map E4) creates classic totes (approx RMB2,700), purses and clutches with top-quality leather in stunning shades, and offers a name engraving service.

# Go for a gentlemanly grooming or suit fitting in the House of Alfred Dunhill

Set back off the road and easy to miss is one of Huaihai Road's most handsome residences, the **Twin Villas**. These almost identical neoclassical stone mansions were built by a Chinese property mogul; the eastern one in 1921 and its conjoined twin in 1927. After a decade lying dormant, the property was adopted in 2009 by luxury brand conglomerate Richemont Group as their China headquarters. The powerbrokers' playground is envisaged as a new-generation luxury retail experience, combining offices with high-end boutiques and sophisticated lounging. Luxury brand brothers Vacheron Constantin and Alfred Dunhill – both old favourites of the high-end Chinese consumer – occupy separate wings of the mansion, their flagships designed to go beyond regular retail and share the history and spirit of the brands in a mini-museum experience.

For **Alfred Dunhill** that means archival pieces and manly toys in the Travel and Discovery Room, leading up to a custom White Shirt Bar and bespoke tailoring service, plus a traditional gentleman's barber. Murano chandelier-strung **Vacheron Constantin** combines retail and bespoke watch orders with a collector's salon and display area.

The upper levels of the mansions are reserved for the exclusive KFF Club. A good concierge should be able to get you into this decadent members club styled like a European salon.

*Twin Villas; 796 Huaihai Road; www.kee club.com; map G5*

# People-watch at a clutch of quirky cafés

A lingering air of bohemia from its French-occupied heyday makes this trendy neighbourhood ideal for café communing. Shanghai's most charming and quirky cafés line the tree-fringed lanes – the following offering great brews and fascinating people-watching.

Ideal for breakfast or a sweet snack, **Farine Bakery** (Ferguson Lane, 378 Wukang Road; www.farine-bakery.com; map B2), owned by popular Shanghai-based French

restauranteur Franck Pecol, occupies a prime perch on one of Shanghai's prettiest streets. Take a seat at the communal bench on the street-facing terrace to nibble Instagram-worthy patisseries and fine coffee.

For a slice of San Francisco in Shanghai, **Boom Boom Bagels** (39 Anfu Road; tel: 150 2140 8818; map D4) is a tiny but rather hip café that opens out to the sidewalk and serves up loaded bagel sandwiches and Shanghai's best coffee. Hang around for happy hour when workers from the office tower next door stop by for after work beers, with three types of craft ales on tap.

Owned by an Austrian expat, **Vienna Café** (25 Shaoxing Road; map G3) has a chic European ambience, and coffees and cakes that are as good as those found in its namesake city.

Next door is one of Shanghai's most cultured cafés. Opened in 1996, the **Old China Hand Reading Room** (27 Shaoxing Road; map G3) is stuffed with antiques and shelves lined with literature, including several tomes recording Shanghai's heritage architecture photographed by café owner Deke Erh. As befits its vintage ambiance, there is no Wi-Fi in this one.

# Hop on a bike or motorcycle sidecar and pootle around the leafy streets and lanes

There's no better way to explore the flat, leafy streets and lanes of the former French Concession than by bicycle. For decades, pedal power was the traditional mode of transport in Shanghai and, with the city streets becoming increasingly choked by motor traffic, it often gets you from A to B faster than a car or bus.

**China Cycle Tours** rents a variety of good quality bikes – city, mountain, touring, tandem, folding and children's – along with helmets and baby seats. They'll also give you free safety advice and a street map, and can deliver bikes to your hotel for an extra fee. Alternatively, you can join one of CCT's guided tours of the city.

If negotiating the crazy Shanghai streets alone is too daunting (drivers are notoriously unpredict-able), then **Insiders Experience** offers tours in vintage motorcycle sidecars. The fabulous Changjiang 750cc's were formerly used by the People's Liberation Army. Expat drivers double as tour guides as they motor one or two passengers around the city's most picturesque routes at a leisurely 25km/hour. Groups travel in packs of between one and three motorcycles, with a capacity of 30 bikes, making for a traffic-stopping spectacle. Helmets, Chinese army coats and rain clothes are provided. For an extra RMB200 they'll even pack a bottle of chilled champagne in the boot.

*China Cycle Tours; www.chinacycletours. com; map page 48, B4*
*Insiders Experience; tel: 138 1761 6975; http://insidersexperience.com; map E4*

# Wake up to breakfast, Shanghai-style, from the city's most popular streetside hawkers

Celebrity chef Jean Georges Vongerichten once famously declared that Shanghai *jian bing* was 'the best breakfast in the world'. During his frequent trips to cook in his namesake restaurant in Shanghai, Jean Georges is often found chowing down on these savoury pancakes at breakfast markets across town.

Although the hygiene standards of many street food vendors may make some stomachs turn, the long lines of locals queuing up for their favourite morning snack attest to their deliciousness. Most neighbourhood fruit and vegetable markets have streetside

breakfast vendors nearby, set up on tricycles or in hole-in-the-wall dwellings. All the dishes are cooked to order and designed to keep you full until lunchtime.

Popular savoury breakfast snacks include long dough crullers *(you tiao)*; fried dumplings filled with pork and broth *(shengjian mantou)*; silken tofu with soy sauce and condiments *(dou hua)*; and freshly steamed buns stuffed with meat, vegetables or red bean paste *(baozi)*. The stand-out is the *jian bing*, a kind of Chinese breakfast burrito. Cooked on a drum-shaped grill, the thin, crispy pancake is topped with a fresh egg, coriander, chives, a dash of fermented soybean sauce and a salty cruller. It is then wrapped up and eaten on the go, usually washed down with a cup of warm soy bean milk.

Breakfast sellers do a roaring trade in the ramshackle, open-fronted cafés on the corner of Xiangyang Road and Changle Road (map E5); near the intersection of Wulumuqi Road and Fuxing Road (map D3); and in front of the wet market on the corner of Yanqing Road by Donghu Road (map E4). Be sure to rise early as these vendors and their snacks usually disappear by 10am.

# Chill out at the coolest live music venues, from jazz to folk to Chinese rock

While the live music scene in Shanghai doesn't rival Beijing's in scope and lifespan, it's still possible to have a great night out and hear some quality music.

Jazz lovers should head straight to **JZ Club** (46 Fuxing Road West, near Yongfu Road; daily 8pm–2am; map C3), which is something of a benchmark for jazz, soul and blues in Shanghai and hosts live performances every night. Velvet curtains and low lighting gives a seductive, old-time vibe.

Just down the street is the smoky **Cotton Club** (1416 Huaihai Middle Road, near Fuxing Road West; Tue–Sun 7.30pm–1.30am; map D3) – the longest established jazz venue in the city. Catering to a slightly grittier crowd, its house band takes to the stage nightly, along with visiting international players.

Also in the neighbourhood, **Heyday** (50 Tai'an Road; tel: 6236 6075; http://heydayjazz.cn; daily 6.30pm–2am; map B2) is a throwback to Shanghai's famed 1930s jazz era. The intimate, fan-shaped bar hosts a nightly roster of Shanghai's leading jazz musicians from 9.30pm, accompanied by barrel-aged classic cocktails.

If rock and punk are more your thing, try **MAO Livehouse** (3/F,

308 Chongqing Road South, near Jianguo Middle Road; open for performances; map H3), run by the folks behind the iconic Beijing venue. China's ever-growing pool of rock and punk bands play regularly, with shows raising the roof most weekends.

A more low-key spot to hear decent live music is **Dada** (115 Xingfu Road, near Fahuazhen Road; 8pm–late; off map, B2) in the west of the district. Tucked away down a side street, it's a magnet for city's hipsters, indie kids and musicians, especially at weekends when live rock bands or DJs play to a packed house.

# Eat your way around China from Hunan to Hong Kong at the best regional restaurants

As a city of immigrants, Shanghai's restaurants represent a veritable microcosm of China. Along with the major cuisines – Cantonese, Beijing, Sichuan – are endless variations in between.

Sichuan's seductive flavours are no stranger to the West – it's the spicy one. At **Sichuan Citizen** (30 Donghu Road; tel: 5404 1235; Mon–Fri noon–9pm, Sat–Sun noon–9.30pm; map E4), the crimson chilli oil matches the comfy chairs and paper lanterns. Book ahead or be prepared to wait at peak hours for the well-priced plates of beef in tongue-numbing chilli oil, *yuxiang* pork, thinly sliced lotus root and house-speciality cold noodles. Be sure to wash it all down with their signature basil drop martinis.

The only thing numbing at **Guyi**

### Shanghainese cooking

Shanghai's own cuisine has its roots in hearty peasant cooking, with none of the grand flavour statements and enormous variety or subtle complexities of Cantonese or Sichuan food. With its long-simmered stews and sauces, sweetened for the child in all of us, this is comfort food, not haute cuisine. An insistence on seasonality and freshness lifts it from the ordinary.

(87 Fumin Road; tel: 6249 5628; daily 11.30am–midnight; map D5) is the wait. This wildly popular Hunan restaurant doesn't accept reservations after 6.30pm, so come early – or late. The décor is contemporary and the packed house an even mix of local and foreign, but the chefs are undoubtedly pure of Hunan heart. Order a plate of cum-in-crusted spareribs and anything made with the central province's smoked bacon (a stir-fry with sour pickled beans is tops).

Despite the shared affinity for cumin, Xinjiang cuisine is a world away. The cool loft space of **Xibo** (3/F, 83 Changshu Road; tel: 5403 8330; daily noon–2.30pm, 6pm–midnight; map D4) eschews the standard 'Gold is Great' design ethos of restaurants from China's westernmost province for a more subtle approach. Cultural artefacts from Xinjiang's ethnic kaleidoscope (Uighur, Tajik, Kazakh, Hui, Kyrgyz, and the owner's own Xibo) serve as the backdrop for a cuisine centered on lamb, *nang* bread, and Silk Road spices.

The Xibo people originated in northeastern China, before an emperor recognised their archery skills and sent them to defend Xinjiang's western frontier, but you won't find any northern-style dumplings in their cuisine these days. For that, it's off to **Dongbei Four Seasons Dumpling King** (1791 Huaihai Middle Road; tel: 6433 0349; daily 11am–3pm, 5–11pm; map B2) whose name tells most of the story: there are 16 types of dumpling on offer. Down-market (though delicious) to some, it's not the place for a date.

If you're looking to meet some-one, **Cha's** (30 Sinan Road; tel: 6093 2062; daily 11am–1.30am; map G5) could be the place. This retro Cantonese diner is so popular that small groups are often obliged to share a table. The 1950s Hong Kong set-piece feel (it's owned by a film director) is upstaged only

by the excellent takes on southern Chinese comfort food, served until 1am: soy-sauce chicken, scallops with broccoli, and the half-tea, half-coffee milk tea known as yin yang – Hong Kong in a cup.

Not forgetting the sweet, oily delights of local cuisine, **Nanling** (168 Yueyang Road; tel: 6467 7381; daily 11am–2pm; map E2) is an old-school institution serving Shang-hainese and Yangzhou favourites. The decor is nothing to write home about, but the crabmeat silken tofu and 'lion's head' pork rissoles are. If you wish to try their nod-to-the-north Peking duck, order it in advance when you book.

# Visit the historic residences of Sun Yat-sen and Zhou Enlai, then relax in lovely Fuxing Park

During the early part of the 20th century, Sinan Road's grand estates housed a veritable who's who of the rich, powerful and revered. Socialites, politicians, intellectuals, artists and the odd gangster lived side by side, including two unlikely neighbours: former Chinese Premier Zhou Enlai and revolutionary leader Dr Sun Yat-sen.

The late Chinese Premier **Zhou Enlai's former residence** stands beneath a tangle of ivy at No. 73. The house's peaceful gardens and spartan rooms once inhabited by leading Communist party figures, are open free to the public. From the upstairs street-facing rooms you look out to a deserted villa on

the opposite side of the road (No. 70). This used to be the Shanghai Maternity and Children's Hospital – and was also a KMT Intelligence Agency base that sent daily reports of the activities in the house.

A few doors away is the modest pebbledash **former residence of Dr Sun Yat-sen** and his wife Soong Qingling (see page 163). Sun Yat-sen was the first leader of the Nationalist Party (KMT) and was elected acting President of China in 1912. He and his powerful wife lived in the two-storey house from 1918 to 1924, and it was here that Dr Sun met with representatives of the Chinese Communist Party to discuss co-operative activities between the parties. The museum depicts the house as Madame Soong decorated it, complete with original furniture, books, glasses and manuscripts.

Dr Sun's house overlooks **Fuxing Park**, called French Park when it opened on Bastille Day in 1909. It's a delightful spot to retreat to after your Sinan Road explorations.

*Former residence of Zhou Enlai; 73 Sinan Road; 9am–4pm; free; map H4*
*Former residence of Dr Sun Yat-sen; 7 Xiangshan Road; daily 9am–4pm; charge; map H4*
*Fuxing Park; 2 Gaolan Road; map H4*

# Delight in the elegant interiors of a French mansion and watch folk artists at work

The **Shanghai Museum of Arts and Crafts** is dedicated to traditional local folk arts and their preservation for future generations. The delightful museum is housed in a beautiful whitewashed French villa (1905). Designed by prolific Hungarian architect Ladislaus Hudec for a powerful French official, it was later home to Shanghai's first mayor, Chen Yi.

Established here in 1960, the three-storey museum exhibits folk arts from the last several decades and also acts as a research institute, workshop and training centre for aspiring artists. The villa is divided into different rooms for different disciplines, including jade, ivory and wood carving on the second floor, embroidery, and costume-making on the third floor, and paper-cutting, lantern-making and ink brush painting on the ground floor. The prized creations exhibited in glass cases are interesting enough, but the main appeal is the ability to roam freely around the artist studios, just off the main exhibition halls, and watch creators of all ages at work. They are generally happy to answer questions or demonstrate techniques for the occasional visitor who wanders through.

The house itself is also a huge draw. Well-preserved interiors allow a rare view of original period detailing in the parquet floors, marble fireplaces, elaborate ceiling moldings and spiraling marble staircase. You can purchase the artists' works from the stores on the ground floor.

*Shanghai Museum of Arts and Crafts; 79 Fenyang Road; tel: 6431 4074; daily 9am–4.30pm; map E3*

# Indulge your sweet tooth at Shanghai's most decadent dessert emporiums

Chocolate lovers are in for a real treat in Shanghai. Leading the charge is Malaysian pastry chef Brian Tan, whose light-textured but rich desserts, truffles and cocktails are available at **Hof** (Sinan Road; map G5) just off Huaihai Road. The heart-pumping menu selection includes chocolate mousse cake flecked with butter-crunch, creamy gelatos and Valrhona hot chocolates. By evening, the carob-toned café morphs into a boutique dessert, wine and cocktail lounge. The Cacao Cocktail is potent but not overly-sweet, served with lime to balance the intense cacao, while the Shanghai Mei Mei mixes vodka, waxberry juice, lime rose and syrup. Tan's exquisite bitter chocolate truffles spiked with Chinese ingredients, like goji berry, green tea and osmanthus also make great gourmet souvenirs.

**CH2 by Whisk** (1250 Huaihai Middle Road; tel: 5404 7770; map E4) offers a full dinner menu with a focus on cheese and oysters, but the real reason people pack this low-key café is its slabs of rich chocolate nut brownie, straw-busting white chocolate thickshakes and other decadent desserts. Singaporean chain **Awfully Chocolate** (Suite 233, B2/F, IAPM Mall, 999 Huaihai Middle Road) also deserves a mention for its heavy balls of dark chocolate ice cream and whole chocolate cakes.

For tempting Asian style desserts, head to Hong Kong's **Honeymoon Dessert** (www.honeymoon-dessert.com) which has several branches throughout Shanghai. Made from nutritious ingredients like red and green beans, sesame, nuts, Thai black rice, sago and tofu, these sweet soups and puddings taste better than they sound – especially the signature Mango Pomelo and Sago Sweet Soup.

# Become a wok wizard and learn some favourite local dishes at a Chinese cooking school

Can't imagine how you'll survive without Shanghai dumplings or hand-pulled noodles once you leave China? Happily, you don't have to. **The Kitchen At...Huaihai Lu** teaches you the techniques behind preparing your favourite Chinese dishes with hands-on classes in different cuisines.

Founded by a professional hotel chef and an event marketing guru in 2007, the school is located in a 19th-century French Concession home that has been fitted out with a large, well-equipped kitchen for group cooking and a cosy dining space for sampling the results of your efforts. There's even a small garden planted with fresh herbs.

Ninety-minute classes led by professional chefs from five-star hotel kitchens are held throughout the week covering a range of cuisines and styles. All skill levels are welcome and the multilingual chefs switch between Chinese and English depending on the class. It's very hands-on – so be prepared to roll up your sleeves and start chopping and stirring.

Each class generally covers two or three recipes that you can re-create at home. As well as mastering specialised cooking techniques, you'll get to explore China's best-known cuisines, from refined Cantonese, to spice-laden Sichuan and the sweeter Shanghainese flavours as you prepare dishes like hot and sour soup, bitter melon braised with pork sparerib in a claypot, and soft tofu with hairy crab meat. There's also a special Shanghai Dumpling and Dim Sum making course.

If you wish to expand your repertoire, The Kitchen At...Huaihai Lu also conducts cooking classes in a wide range of global cuisines, including Italian, Spanish, French, Mexican, Japanese and Thai. Check their website for the latest schedules.

*The Kitchen At...Huaihai Lu; Building 20, 3/F, 383 Xiangyang Road South; tel: 6433 2700; www.thekitchenat.com; map F2*

# Explore the eco-enclave Jiashan Market then join the street party on Yongkang Road

One of the joys of exploring Shanghai's old residential lanes, or *longtang*, is the myriad surprises and contrasts they contain. Deep inside one lane off Shaanxi Road, past a lively local street market of vendors selling seafood and vegetables, is one such surprise: a friendly eco-community known as **Jiashan Market**.

Brainchild of Shanghai-based urban design firm BAU, disillusioned with the 'churning out' of modern Chinese neighbourhoods with an emphasis on fast-paced change rather than thoughtful planning and sustainability, they envisaged Jiashan Market as an Environmentally Sustainable Design (ESD) to showcase the benefits of an urban garden community.

Originally the Shanghai Knitting Factory compound, the warehouses have been transformed into loft residences, offices and restaurants, surrounding an open-air courtyard and barbecue pavilion. Residents and visitors can grab an organic snack or Yunnan coffee at **Melange Oasis cafe** or sample mod-Malay flavours at **Café Sambal**. Fresh fruits, vegetables, herbs and other ingredients come courtesy of the mini organic farms on the buildings' rooftops – which also help insulate the building, reduce energy consumption and shrink the carbon footprint of this neat little enclave. They also have a monthly eco market in the courtyard.

From here, it's a short stroll to Yongkang Road, a narrow street lined with tiny bars, taquerías and coffee shops. Each venue has sidewalk seating and when the weather is fine a street party atmosphere ensues. Until 10pm that is, when tense relations with the upstairs neighbours means everyone has to quieten down and move inside.

*Jiashan Market; No. 37, Lane 550 Shaanxi Road South; http://jiashanmarket.com; map F3*
*Yongkang Road, between Jianshan Road and Xiangyang Road; map F3*

# Visit some of the French Concession's most progressive contemporary art galleries

Though People's Square is home to Shanghai's prominent galleries such as the Museum of Contemporary Art, the lanes of the former French Concession contain some of the most cutting edge art spaces in the city. International ownership means these smaller galleries have links with the European and American art spheres, so they draw acclaimed names from both the East and West.

Hidden down a quiet lane, the **James Cohan Gallery** is in a crumbling European-style villa surrounded by a quaint garden of lush greenery and shaded benches. Spread over three rooms, the exhibition space is full of light with whitewashed walls and antique floorboards – perfect for showing the works of artists such as Alex Katz and Louise Bourgeois, who have had shows here.

Five minutes walk from James Cohan in the swanky Surpass Court (home to trendy bars, upscale restaurants and shops) **Art Labor** is one of the more progressive galleries in Shanghai. The space's exposed concrete, spot-lighting and ceiling pipes provide an industrial chic backdrop for shows from both international and local artists.

One of the smallest exhibition spaces in the city, **Leo Gallery** is

also one of the most charming. In trendy Ferguson Lane, the two-floor gallery is in a converted villa with a sun-dappled rooftop terrace for pit-stops. Past exhibitions have included the bright oil paintings of Basmat Levin and sculptures from Kevin Fung.

*Art Labor; Building 4, 570 Yongjia Road; tel: 3460 5331; www.artlaborgallery.com; Tue–Sun 11am–7pm; free; map E2*
*James Cohan Gallery; Building 1, Lane 170 Yueyang Road; tel: 5466 0825; www.james cohan.com; Tue–Sun 11am–6pm; free; map E2*
*Leo Gallery; Ferguson Lane, 374–376 Wukang Road; tel: 5464 8785; www.leo gallery.com.cn; Tue–Sun 11am–7pm; free; map B2*

# Discover Communist-era art at the Propaganda Poster Art Centre

Shanghai's future-focused energies overshadow contemplation of its more recent history. This hidden museum in a basement apartment is a treasure trove of retro China from the 1950s–70s. The museum was created by Shanghai local Yang Pei Ming to preserve and showcase Mao-era propaganda artworks. Over the years, he amassed a collection of more than 5,000 posters, book covers, newspaper ads and artefacts exhorting China to achieve monumental national feats fuelled by the glory of Mao's ideological vision. The poster images depict peasants, workers, schoolchildren and 'model Communists' pulling together for the greater good of the motherland, with phrases such as the ubiquitous 'The East is Red'. Mao himself is deified in several ways, often with beams of sunlight radiating through his body, or in heroic poses speaking to the Chinese people.

The style and detail of the Communist Party posters change significantly from the 1949 Communist Revolution to Mao's death in 1976, although the dominating themes remained Communism's superiority, the wolfish aggression of Western capitalism and the benefits of universal brotherhood in China.

This skillfully curated exhibition is a unique chronology of these changes during an era of colourful, yet crudely socially manipulative, mass propaganda. Some of the posters, plus a collection of memorabilia, are available for purchase in the museum shop.

*Propaganda Poster Art Centre; Room B-0C, 868 Huashan Road; tel: 6211 1845; www.shanghaipropagandaart.com; daily 10am–5pm; map B4*

### Maomentoes

More Mao memorabilia can be found at Madame Mao's Dowry (207 Fumin Road; tel: 5403 3551), a fun boutique selling original revolution-era posters, photographs, woodblock prints and paintings, along with their own hand-painted accessories with updated slogans, like 'Defend Our Stock Exchange'.

# Craft and glaze your own Chinese porcelain at the Pottery Workshop

For a deeper insight into traditional Chinese ceramic-making, get your hands dirty at the **Pottery Workshop**. This ceramics studio started in a Hong Kong basement over 25 years ago has expanded to four Chinese cities – including Jingdezhen, the ancient porcelain capital of China where the imperial kilns were located. The Pottery Workshop's in-house and guest ceramicists create funky handmade bowls, tea sets, sculptures and more that are for sale in its two Shanghai boutiques. Beyond this, they also have an education centre offering a variety of classes in both pottery and sculpture, and even professional artist residencies in Jingdezhen. From the basics of hand building and using the pottery wheel to more challenging sessions in aesthetic development, hand painting and techniques such as mould-making, the experienced teachers conduct classes in English and Mandarin for up to 20 students at a time. Classes are available for all ages, with the creative junior classes (5–14 years) a real hit, allowing kids to craft their own figurines, masks, rockets and animals.

Be sure to wear clothes that you can get dirty or bring your own apron. Classes include materials, basic tools and a firing fee.

*The Pottery Workshop; No. 1A Lane Shaanxi Road South; tel: 6445 0902; www.potteryworkshop.com.cn; map F5*

# PUDONG

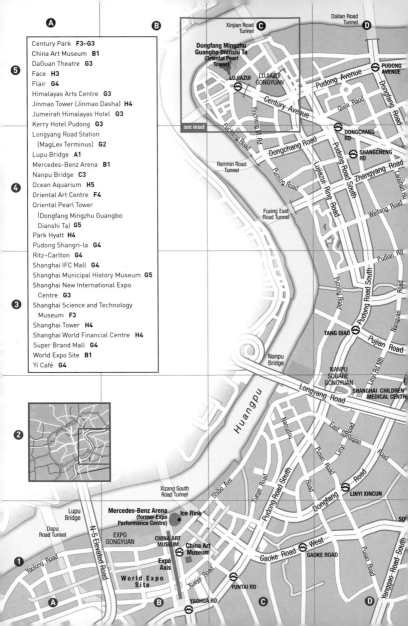

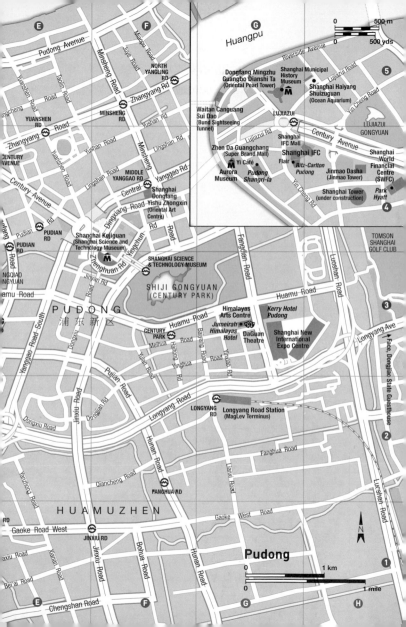

# Scale the heights of Shanghai's skytowers and take in heartstopping views

In the early 1990s, the Shanghai government announced plans to build three monumental sky-scrapers on a triangle of land in Pudong, symbolising the status of the district as a rising global financial centre. Two decades later, the triptych proudly dominates the Pudong skyline. The 88-level Jinmao Tower opened in 1999, the 101-floor Shanghai World Financial Centre followed in 2008 and topping these super-tall siblings, the 121-floor Shanghai Tower was unveiled in 2015.

Echoing elements of Shanghai's 1930s Art Deco heritage and a silhouette of Chinese pagodas, the glistening tiered pinnacle of **Jinmao Tower**, designed by Skidmore, Owings and Merrill, quickly became a cherished Shanghai landmark. China's tallest building at the time made headlines in June 2007, when French urban climber Alain Robert, sporting a Spiderman costume, scaled the exterior and was promptly arrested by police.

The Jinmao Tower comprises office floors, convention facilities, the J-Life retail complex and the Grand Hyatt hotel from the 53rd to the 87th floors. The 88th-floor Observatory affords magnificent vistas. One floor below, Shanghai's original sky lounge, the Grand Hyatt's Cloud 9 bar, yields similar 360-degree views – but with the added benefit of cosy armchairs and classy cocktails.

Nicknamed the 'bottle opener' because of its rectangular opening at the top, the Japanese Mori-built **Shanghai World Financial Centre** (SWFC) was designed by Kohn Pedersen Fox. Occupying this extraordinary structure are retail and dining on the basement and ground levels, multiple office floors and the Park Hyatt Shanghai between the 79th and 93rd floors. Most exciting of all is the vertigo-inducing SWFC Observatory, featuring three above-the-clouds observation platforms. The crowning glory is the 100th-floor Sky Walk 100 – a 55 metre (180ft)-long glass corridor overhanging the trapezoidal gap at the building's summit. Transparent inset floor panels enable visitors, quite literally, to look almost half a kilometre (a third of a mile) down to the city below.

Miraculously dwarfing its super-tall siblings, the **Shanghai Tower**, designed by US-based architectural firm Gensler, stands a staggering 632 metres (2,073ft) tall, making it the second-tallest building on earth.

Its tapered spiraling form, said to resemble a dragon's tail, rotates 120-degrees from base to top, the optimal amount to minimise wind loads in this typhoon prone city. Wrapping around the exterior is a glass curtain wall comprising more than 20,000 panels of different shapes, one of 43 sustainable innovations in this LEED Gold-certified green building. Inside, a series of vertically stacked sky gardens (a third of the site is green space) are home to offices, shops, the luxurious J Hotel and the world's highest observatory on the 119th floor. The fastest elevators on the planet whisk visitors to the top at speeds exceeding 18m/sec (40mph) and the exterior lighting is powered by 270 wind turbines built into the façade.

*Shanghai World Financial Centre; Dongtai Road; tel: 4001 100 555; www.swfc-observatory.com; daily 8am–11pm, last entry 10pm; charge; map H4*
*Jinmao Tower; 88 Century Avenue; tel: 5047 6688; www.jinmao88.com; daily 8.30am–10pm; map H4*
*Shanghai Tower; 501 Yincheng Middle Road; 3383 1088; map C4*

# Sip a sunset cocktail on the cloud-view terrace of Flair

When the elevator doors open after the ear-popping ride to the 58th floor of the Shanghai IFC Tower, it's not unusual to find a TV crew waiting to descend. Seemingly floating on a cloud above Shanghai, **Flair** has become the go-to destination for broadcast interviews using the cityscape as a backdrop. The vistas really are jaw-dropping. Elevated high above the Pudong riverbank, the cherry spheres of the Oriental Pearl Tower appear almost touchable, and on a clear evening the neon lights stretch to the horizon. Consequently, memories – and not just TV shows – are recorded here daily. Flair is Shanghai's hottest 'see-and-be-photographed' destination. But don't expect to ascend, snap and descend – seats on the terrace are in demand, so be sure to reserve a table in advance. The optimum time to take your seat is just before sunset, so that you have a drink in hand, and a plate of nibbles to munch on, when the burning orange sun sinks behind the Bund.

Flair is more than just a high-rise lounge – it serves very good pan-Asian tapas, inside the restaurant and on the split-level outdoor terrace. There's no finer way to usher in Shanghai nightfall than with a Flair Experience cocktail (Jameson Whiskey, Absolut Pears Vodka, mango puree, peach syrup and ginger) and a table spread of pan-seared fois gras with miso rice, pomelo salad with kaffir lime dressing, and drunken Manila crab with ginger and spring onion. Just remember to pack your camera.

*Flair; 58/F, The Ritz-Carlton Pudong, IFC Tower, 8 Century Avenue; tel: 2020 1888; www.ritzcarlton.com; map G4*

# Fly through thin air at dizzying speed aboard the levitating MagLev train

Since 2010, China's nationwide rollout of its high-speed, inter-city train network has grabbed global headlines, but back in 2004 Shanghai sat at the forefront of the nation's rail upgrade ambitions. The opening of the magnetic levitation (MagLev) line earned Shanghai boasting rights for having the world's fastest passenger train.

Admittedly, the MagLev serves a limited purpose, running only on a 30km (19-mile) route between Shanghai Pudong International Airport and Longyang Road station (map G2) in Pudong, which is a transit point for Metro Lines 2, 7 and 16. But this is a truly thrilling ride. The 8-minute journey averages 240km/h (149mph), and reaches a top speed – at which point myriad digital cameras are hoisted towards the in-carriage speedometer – of 431km/h (267mph). It is like being strapped to a bullet.

The world's first commercial MagLev line uses 'contactless technology' devised by Germany's Transrapid company. The train is elevated by powerful magnets about 10mm above the purpose-built track, called a guideway, as it 'guides' rather than 'directs' the train's movement. Other magnets provide propulsion and braking.

MagLev trains attain higher speeds and require less maintenance than conventional high-speed trains because no friction exists. There are rumours of plans to extend the MagLev line to connect Shanghai's two airports, Pudong and Hongqiao. The 55km (34-mile) journey would take around 15 minutes. The MagLev is not considered economically viable for inter-city travel because the initial development costs are prohibitively high – Transrapid's technology was specifically created for short journeys.

*Trains run daily every 15–20 minutes, 6.45am–9.40pm; for ticket and fare information go to www.smtdc.com/en*

# Dine, drink and spend big at Shanghai IFC, the city's smartest shopping hub

Two of Pudong's smartest mega malls face off in the heart of Lujiazui, the east riverbank's glitzy commercial centre. **Shanghai IFC Mall**, which opened in 2010, occupies the central podium of Cesar Pelli's IFC twin towers. Enveloped in a signature scent and playing piped classical concertos, the six-level mall is home to multi-storey boutiques including Cartier,

Ferragamo, Prada *et al.*, as well as more affordable brands like Miss Sixty and Diesel. You can pick up picnic supplies at the excellent City Super(market) at LG2 on your way to Century Park (see page 124).

Dining options include Cali-Japanese sushi at Haiku by Hatsune and Italian stunner Isola Bar & Grill. In addition to opulent dining rooms, the fourth floor restaurants are blessed with stunning terraces overlooking the frenetic consumer action below. Plenty of Japanese fast-food chains and coffee shops can be found on the lower levels.

Opposite the IFC is China's largest mall, **Superbrand Mall**. This heaving retail behemoth contains 13 storeys of high-street labels. More surprising inclusions are an Egyptian-themed Cineplex, KTV rooms and an ice-skating rink. Several cafes and bars fringe the mall on the ground level – Element Fresh is a great place to stop for a refreshing smoothie or head to Blue Frog for something stronger.

*Shanghai IFC Mall; 8 Century Avenue; tel: 2020 7000; www.shanghaiifc.com.cn; map G4*
*Super Brand Mall; 168 Lujiazui Road West; tel: 6887 7888; www.superbrandmall.com; map G4*

# Marvel at Buddhist sculptures and other Chinese antiquities in the dazzling waterfront Aurora Museum

It's easy to spot the Aurora Building on the Pudong waterfront – it's the reflective gold one that flashes 'I Love Shanghai' by night. At its base, in a 'sapphire curio box' designed by famed Japanese architect Tadao Ando, is the less well known – but splendid – Aurora Museum.

The custom-built private museum by Taiwan's Aurora Group showcases their astounding collection of jade, terracotta figurines, porcelain and Buddhist sculptures, with a research centre promoting the preservation of archaeology and antiquities.

Defined by a monochrome palette and sleek contemporary angles, the exhibition levels are each devoted to a different theme and spliced through with an atrium that allows light to influence the spaces in interesting ways.

The first level focuses on ancient pottery figurines unearthed from burial tombs between the Han and Tang dynasties (206BC–907AD). Multimedia 3D projections and a theatrical gong and zither soundtrack bring the apricot-hued pieces to life.

Ascending the spiral staircase, a collection of jade spanning 8,000 years is showcased in dark-green display cases, and stunning blue and white porcelain pieces stand atop translucent glowing pedestals.

The top level is reserved for ancient Buddhist statuary, overseen by the serene gaze of a 2.3-metre-tall wooden Guanyin Bodhisattva. Dating from the Eastern Han dynasty (25–220AD), the stone, wood, clay and bronze statues portray the Sinicization of Buddhist art, with features becoming more Oriental in appearance over the millennia.

Vying for attention on the upper levels is a horizontal strip of windows affording fine vantages of the Bund buildings across the river. Shanghai's combination of classic and modern skylines further enhances the Aurora Museum's immersive journey into China's ancient cultural history.

*Aurora Museum; 99 Fucheng Road; tel: 5840 8899; www.auroramuseum.cn, Tues–Sun 10am–5pm (open until 9pm on Fridays); RMB60 entrance; map C5*

# Savour local Chinese cuisine and exquisite river views

Combining a fine Chinese meal with a side serving of Huangpu river views makes for a memorable gourmet experience. Fortunately, several popular local restaurants have outposts in Pudong's riverside malls.

**Shanghai Min** (9/F, Super Brand Mall; tel: 5047 2219) started as a small local diner with just four tables in 1987. It now has more than 30 restaurants across Asia serving upscale Shanghainese cuisine. Tasty dishes to choose on the encyclopedic menu include the Organic Vegetable Salad with Secret Sauce, Chicken Marinated with Chinese Rice Wine and Grandma's Meat Pot.

Taiwanese diner **Din Tai Fung** (Rm 24, 3/F, Super Brand Mall; tel: 5047 8882) serves well-executed Chinese favourites in a bright, airy dining room with large windows looking out to Pudong. Be sure to order their signature pork and crabmeat *xiaolongbao* dumplings – or if you're feeling extra fancy, go for the delicious truffle version.

**South Beauty** (10/F, Superbrand Mall; tel: 5047 1917) is another gourmet emporium with designer dining rooms across the city. This outpost is beautifully styled with emerald green glass, striking scarlet armchairs, water channels and an open kitchen specialising in refined Sichuan and Cantonese cuisine. The wraparound 10th-floor river views are as jaw-dropping as the food is tongue-numbingly spicy.

If you prefer the flavours of Canton, **Lei Garden** (3/F, Shanghai IFC Mall, 8 Century Avenue; tel: 5106 1688) is a branch of the Michelin-star winning Hong Kong institution. Order top-sellers like the baby duck and speciality soups a day in advance. Roasted meats and superb dim sum are other reasons to go – and of course views over Lujiazui from the third floor.

*Super Brand Mall and Shanghai IFC Mall: map G4. See page 118 for details*

# Visit China's answer to the Eiffel Tower: the China Art Museum

From London's Crystal Palace, built to host the first Great Exhibition in 1851, to the Eiffel Tower in Paris in 1889 and the Brussels Atomium in 1958, through the ages, the World Fair has bequeathed its hosts with notable structures – the most outstanding of which become a symbol of that city.

Standing 63 metres (207ft) in height – three times the height of any other national pavilion – the bright red **China Pavilion** was the centrepiece of the 2010 World Expo, which garnered a record 73 million visitors.

The eye-popping design is notable for its traditional roof, said to represent an emperor's crown and made of 56 interlocking *dougong* wooden brackets fixed layer upon layer between the top of a column and a crossbeam. This style of architecture is said to date back more than 2,000 years.

After a two-year refit, the iconic building was reopened in 2012 as the **China Art Museum** (also known as the China Art Palace). Showcasing the world's biggest collection of modern Chinese art, it covers 640,000 sqm across five levels.

More than 600 artworks by iconic 20th-century painters like Wu Guanzhong and Qi Baishi hang alongside Chinese calligraphy and ink brush paintings, propaganda art and socialist-realist sculptures, charting the development of modern art in China since the late Qing Dynasty. There are also halls devoted to the Shanghai Film Animation Studio and high-profile visiting exhibitions from the likes of the British Museum and the Whitney.

Take the colourful ramp between the top two floors for wraparound views of the Shanghai skyline through the red frame of the inverted pyramid, dubbed the 'Crown of the East'. The far-flung location is easily accessible on the Shanghai Metro, directly above the China Art Museum station on Line 8.

*China Art Palace, Zone A, Pudong Road, near Shangnan Road; tel: 6222 8822; http://artshow.eastday.com; Tue–Sun 9am–5pm; map B1*

# Zoom up the space-age Oriental Pearl Tower for a 360 degree view from one of its spheres

Shanghai's skyline seems to change with startling regularity, but one city veteran has retained its iconic status since 1994. The development of the Pudong waterfront was still in its infancy when the **Shanghai Oriental Pearl Tower** opened after four years of construction. When completed, it was China's tallest building, although it has since been overtaken by a handful of urban skyscrapers – notably its near neighbour, the 101-storey Shanghai World Financial Centre. It is, however, the world's fourth tallest telecommunications tower, after the Canton Tower in Guangzhou, Toronto's CN Tower and Moscow's Ostankino Tower.

A series of gleaming silver and cranberry-coloured spheres are laced along the length of the 468-metre (1,535ft) TV tower, which is supported by three 7-metre (23ft) -thick stanchions – giving it the appearance of a space rocket on a launch pad. At night, the spheres are illuminated in electrifying neon kaleidoscopes. The main sightseeing platform is in a large sphere, 263 metres (863ft) above street level. Viewfinder plaques identify the skyline's standout structures to enhance the superb views. A second viewing level – the Space Module – sits in the upper sphere at 350 metres (1,092ft). Five smaller spheres contain a 25-room hotel, while the summit pearl has a rotating restaurant.

The **Shanghai Municipal History Museum** in the basement, features atmospheric recreations of cobble-stoned old Shanghai streets, a gun from the Opium Wars, and the original lions that sat in front of the Hong Kong and Shanghai Bank.

*Oriental Pearl Tower; 1 Century Avenue; tel: 5879 1888; daily 8.30am–9.30pm; charge; map G5*

# Check out Arata Isozaki's feng shui-inspired Himalayas Arts Centre

Pudong boasts many an experimental building, but lacked fine arts spaces. So the locally based Zendai Property Group decided to combine the two in one ambitious project. The owners of Pudong's acclaimed Zendai Museum of Modern Art have transferred the collection to the Himalayas Art Museum within the dramatic new **Himalayas Art Centre**, which it calls an 'archisculptural masterpiece for 21st century China'.

Japanese architect Arata Isozaki, famed for his work on the 1992 Barcelona Olympic Stadium and the Los Angeles Museum of Contemporary Art, designed the Himalayas Centre, which is infused with feng shui and eastern structural principles. Echoing elements of Gaudi's Modernist buildings in Barcelona, the uneven exterior design represents an 'organic forest' of irregularly shaped holes carved into the walls rising from the ground to symbolise tree trunks.

The **Shanghai Himalayas Museum** presents an eclectic collection that includes ancient Dunhuang frescoes, Yamato-e Japanese paintings based on China's Tang dynasty scroll-style art, oil paintings by contemporary artists and hand-painted Jingdezhen porcelain.

Also housed within this arresting building are the 1,100-seat **DaGuan Theatre**, an underground retail plaza, and the first Asia-Pacific hotel by Dubai luxury hotel group Jumeirah, in which every artwork, loaned from the owner's personal collection, is an original piece. Take a peek at the hotel lobby, featuring an antique Ming Dynasty wood pavilion that hosts live performances, beneath a 260 sqm LED screen ceiling beaming artsy animations. You can borrow a free iPod art tour to explore the hotel art pieces on display.

*Himalayas Centre; 869 Yinghua Road; tel: 5033 9801; www.himalayasart.cn; Tue–Sun 10am–6pm (open until 9pm on Wed); map G3*

**123**

# Ride a tandem, fly a kite or have a picnic with the locals in the beautifully landscaped Century Park

Although appearances may be deceptive, Shanghai isn't all about skyscrapers, elevated highways and apartment blocks. It's a surprisingly green city if you know where to look. **Century Park** is the largest public green space in the metropolitan area. Acting as a green lung for the city, it is a popular spot for biking, walking and relaxing amid the greenery. Anchored by a huge lake, this beautifully landscaped stretch of parkland rarely feels busy, even at weekends.

Designed by British landscaping firm LUC, Century Park blends Chinese and Japanese styles in the layout of its gardens, lakes and paths as well as grassland and wilderness. Around the lake are several scenic spots, and the perimeter path is popular with joggers.

As well as plenty of attractive scenery to admire and landscapes to explore, the park offers a variety of recreational activities. Visitors can hire boats on the lake, or try their hand at tandem bike-riding along the wide paths and avenues (regular bikes are also available). If it's breezy enough, you can pick up a kite to fly at the park gates.

And if all that physical activity has you gasping for a drink or a bite to eat, there are convenience stores and teahouses dotted around the park.

*Century Park; 1001 Jinxiu Road; tel: 5833 0221; daily 7am–6pm; map F–G3*

# Be a culture vulture at the Oriental Arts Centre or see who's playing the Mercedes-Benz Arena

Though proud of its space-age skyline, Pudong has long struggled with its perception as a cultural wasteland. All the cool culture occurred on the opposite side of the Huangpu River in Puxi. No longer. Two dramatically crafted performance centres have changed the way Shanghai views its east bank.

The **Oriental Arts Centre**, which opened in 2005, led Pudong's cultural charge. Designed by French architect Paul Andreu, it comprises five dark granite-based hemispheroids housing the lobby, performance hall, concert hall, exhibition hall and opera hall. Viewed from above, the building opens out like a flowering butterfly orchid. At night, 880 inlaid lights illuminate the roof to spectacular effect. The Oriental Arts Centre's acclaimed acoustics, contemporary design and varied performance spaces have attracted some of the world's leading philharmonic and chamber orchestras and opera performers. The Saturday brunch chorus and symphony concerts are a good-value way to experience this impressive venue.

In its former guise, the Expo Performance Centre hosted the spectacular opening and closing ceremonies for the 2010 World Expo. After Expo finished, the riverside venue was rechristened the **Mercedes-Benz Arena**, becoming China's first corporate naming rights deal for a major venue. The six-level, 18,000-seat arena stages concerts by Chinese and international popstars, theatrical and dance shows, and sporting events. Within the same complex are Shanghai's biggest ice rink, a six-screen cinema, a nightclub, restaurants and retail outlets. Like the Oriental Art Centre, this oyster-shell building is radiantly lit at night.

*Oriental Art Centre; 425 Dingxiang Road; tel: 6854 1234; www.shoac.com.cn; map F4 Mercedes-Benz Arena; 1200 Expo Avenue; tel: 400 181 6688; www.mercedes-benzarena.com; map B1*

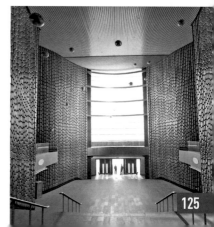

# Indulge your little emperors with Pudong's array of child-friendly attractions

Pudong is a vast residential district and home to Shanghai's finest schools, which means it's a family-friendly place with plenty of activities on offer for kids.

Opened in late 2010, the full-sized indoor **ice rink at the Mercedes-Benz Arena** (see page 125) features a state-of-the-art sound system and colourful lighting effects. Adult-sounding but very kid-friendly, the cavernous **Shanghai Science and Technology Museum** has many intriguing exhibits, including the World of

Robots, Children's Rainbow Land and Space Navigation, plus an IMAX cinema. Nearby, **Century Park** (see page 124) is a popular spot for family kite-flying, roller-blading and Frisbee-throwing at weekends.

On the riverside in front of the Oriental Pearl Tower, the **Shanghai Ocean Aquarium** takes you on an underwater journey via the icy tides of the Antarctic, the rivers of Africa and the rainforests of Southeast Asia. En route you'll encounter sharks, Chinese water dragons, electric eels and jellyfish.

For a sweet treat, visit the extraordinary candy counter at the Pudong Shangri-La's **Yi Café** buffet restaurant. The dessert selection is vast, and kids can also pick up a special sweetbox and fill it with their own colourful pick-and-mix confectionery.

*Shanghai Science and Technology Museum; 2000 Century Boulevard; tel: 6854 2000; www.sstm.org.cn; Tue–Sun 9am–5.15pm; charge; map F3*
*Shanghai Aquarium, 1388 Lujiazui Ring Road; tel: 5877 9988; www.sh-soa.com; 10am–6pm; charge; map H5*
*Yi Café; 2/F, Pudong Shangri-La, 33 Fucheng Road; tel: 5877 5372; www.shangri-la.com; map G4*

# Meet Mickey and friends at the Most Magical Place in Pudong: Shanghai Disney Resort

The much-anticipated **Shanghai Disney Resort** opened in June 2016, becoming the first Disney Resort in mainland China and one of six worldwide.

Predictably, the Shanghai resort unveils several Disney firsts – including the "tallest, largest and most interactive" Enchanted Storybook Castle ever created, complete with a Crystal Grotto hidden beneath.

Covering 3.9 sq km, it consists of a Shanghai Disneyland theme park with six themed lands, a 40-hectare Wishing Star Park and a Disneytown shopping, dining and entertainment district. There is also a Walt Disney Grand Theatre staging the first-ever Mandarin production of Disney's *The Lion King*, plus an Art Nouveau-styled Disneyland hotel and a Toy Story hotel.

Other fun firsts include a thrill-seeking, high-speed TRON Lightcycle Power Run rollercoaster; Treasure Cove, the first-ever pirate-themed land that also includes a Captain Jack Sparrow stunt show; and dinosaur-themed escapades on the premiere Adventure Isle. Visitors can meet and take selfies with their favourite cartoon characters on the longest-ever Disney parade route.

In a nod to local culture, Garden of the Twelve Friends sees the 12 animals of the Chinese zodiac re-imagined as Disney and Pixar characters, while Tomorrowland is inspired by Shanghai's futuristic side, with a Buzz Lightyear space ranger ride and with fun with jet packs. The new happiest place on earth can be found at the end of Metro line 11 in far-flung Pudong.

*Shanghai Disney Resort; 1009 West Shendi Road, Pudong; www.shanghaidisneyresort.com/en*

# SUZHOU CREEK AND NORTHERN DISTRICTS

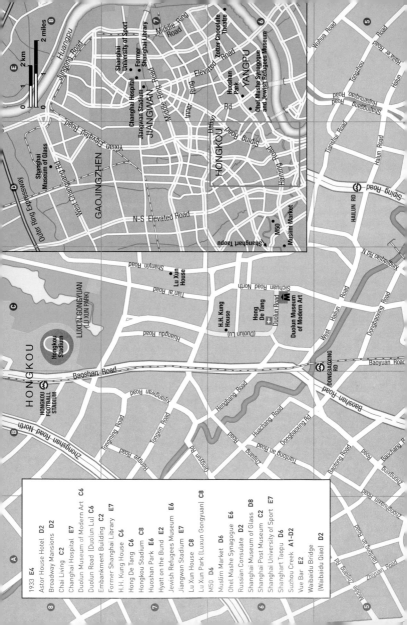

**Legend (index):**

- 1933 **E4**
- Astor House Hotel **D2**
- Broadway Mansions **D2**
- Chai Living **C2**
- Changhai Hospital **E7**
- Duolun Museum of Modern Art **C6**
- Duolun Road (Duolun Lu) **C6**
- Embankment Building **C2**
- Former Shanghai Library **E7**
- H.H. Kung House **C6**
- Hong De Tang **C6**
- Hongkou Stadium **C8**
- Huoshan Park **E6**
- Hyatt on the Bund **E2**
- Jewish Refugees Museum **E6**
- Jiangwan Stadium **E7**
- Lu Xun House **C8**
- Lu Xun Park (Luxun Gongyuan) **C8**
- M50 **D6**
- Muslim Market **D6**
- Ohel Moishe Synagogue **E6**
- Russian Consulate **D2**
- Shanghai Museum of Glass **D8**
- Shanghai Post Museum **C2**
- Shanghai University of Sport **E7**
- Shanghart Taopu **D6**
- Suzhou Creek **A1–D2**
- Vue Bar **E2**
- Waibaidu Bridge (Waibaidu Qiao) **D2**

Map labels visible:

HONGKOU · YANGPU · JIANGWAN · GAOJINGZHEN

HONGKOU FOOTBALL STADIUM · Hongkou Stadium · LUXUN GONGYUAN (LU XUN PARK)

Shanghai Museum of Glass · Shanghai University of Sport · Former Shanghai Library · Shanghai Stadium · Jiangwan Stadium · Changhai Hospital · Middle Ring Road · Elevated Zoter Chocolate Theatre · Ohel Moshe Synagogue and Jewish Refugees Museum · Huoshan Park · M50 · Muslim Market · Shanghart Taopu · Lu Xun House · H.H. Kung House · Hong De Tang · Duolun Museum of Modern Art

Roads: Huangpu · Jinggong Road · West Changjiang Road · Yixian Elevated Road · N-S Elevated Road · Outer Ring Expressway · Zhongshan Road North · Baoshan Road · Baoyuan Road · Middle Ring Road · Dongbaoxing Rd · HAILUN RD · Siping Road · DONGBAOXING RD · Sichuan Road North · Duolun Road · Shanyin Road · Tian'ai Road · Huangdu Road

Scale: 0 — 1 — 2 miles / 0 — 1 — 2 km

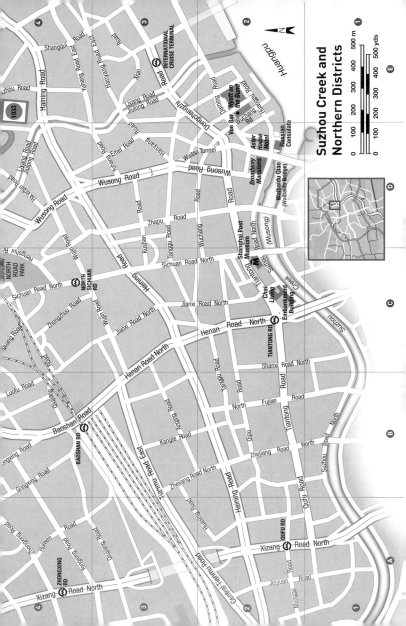

## Suzhou Creek and Northern Districts

Hangpu

1933

INTERNATIONAL CRUISE TERMINAL

Hyatt on the Bund

Vue Bar

Astor House Hotel

Russian Consulate

Broadway Mansions

Waibaidu Qiao (Waibaidu Bridge)

Shanghai Post Museum

Chai Living

Embankment Building

Suzhou Creek

Shangqui Road

Haining Road

zhou Road

Zhoushan Road East

Wuhang Road East

Wuhang Road East

Xian Road

Liyang Road

Jiulong Road

Dongchangzhi Road

Dongdaming Road

Wuchang Rd

Hanyang Road

Haitan Tunnel

Wusong Road

Wusong Road

Wusong Road

Wusong Road

Liyang Road

Jiulong Road

Emei Road

Guang Road

Ha Erbin Road

Hengshui Rd

Zhapu Road

Kushan Road

Tanggu Road

Wuchang Road

Sichuan Road North

Wuhu Road

Zhoushan Road

Tiantong Road

North (Wusong)

Sichuan Road North

Zhongzhou Road

Haining Road

NORTH NORTH ROAD PARK

NORTH SICHUAN RD

Wuhu Road

Jianxi Road North

Jianxi Road North

Henan Road North

Henan Road North

Shanxi Road North

Tiantong Road

TIANTONG RD

Luofu Road

Daming Road

Baoshan Road

BAOSHAN RD

Fujian Road North

Anqing Road

Tanggu Road

Ningbo Road

Suzhou Road North

Qipu Road

Cingxing Road

ngking Road

Cingxing Road

Kangle Road

Zhejiang Road North

Tiantong Road North

Zhejiang Road

North

Suzhou Road North

BAOSHAN ROAD

Tianmu Road East

Haining Road

Huxing Road

Zhongxing Road

Wuwen Road

Hebei Road

QUFU RD

Qufu Road

Xizang Road North

XIZANG Road North

Central Tianmu Hotel

Jinyuan Road

Menggu Road

ZHONGXING RD

Xizang Road North

N

# Follow the literary trail along Duolun Road, 1930s intellectual hub and home to revered writer, Lu Xun

Hongkou district was home to several progressive Chinese writers, artists and intellectuals, who settled around Duolun Road in the 1930s. Most famous of all was Lu Xun (1881–1936), a writer, thinker and revolutionary who is regarded as the father of modern Chinese literature. He was instrumental in founding the League of Leftist Writers in 1930 to 'struggle for proletarian liberation' through writing. The league is commemorated with a small museum in one of the writer's well-preserved houses.

Lu Xun lived out his final years in Hongkou and his legacy is writ large. His plain red-brick Japanese Concession house has been left just as it was when he lived here. **Lu Xun Park** – a delightful green space with lakes, pagodas, and hordes of locals that gather to sing opera and play chess – also contains the writer's tomb, with memorial calligraphy inscribed by Mao Zedong, and the Lu Xun Memorial Hall exhibiting his letters, personal artefacts and photos from the period.

The L-shaped pedestrian stretch of **Duolun Road**, designated a 'cultural street' by the government, is lined with galleries, bookshops, teahouses, antique stores and several heritage buildings, along with bronze statues of famous residents in various states of writerly repose. Highlights of the street include the Hong De Tang, a church built in 1928 with upturned Chinese eaves and red columns, the proud Xi Shi Zhong Lou bell tower, and state-run Shanghai Duolun Museum of Modern Art. Stop for a look at the lavish Moorish-style house at the end of Duolun Road, built in 1924, for financier HH Kung.

*Lu Xun Park: map C8*
*Duolun Road Cultural Celebrities Street: map C6*

# Visit the ghosts of Shanghai's Jewish past at the wartime Ghetto and Jewish Refugees Museum

Surpisingly, there is no other place in the world that saved so many Jewish lives during World War II as Shanghai. Between 1938 and 1940, some 20,000 Jews flooded into the city, which had no visa restrictions at that time.

Shanghai's Jewish presence dates back to the 19th century. Sephardic Jewish families such as the Sassoons, Kadoories and Ezras became powerful developers of real estate, hotels, banking and infrastructure, setting Shanghai on track towards its 'Pearl of the Orient' status. They were followed by Russian Jews in the early 20th century, who arrived via the trans-Siberian rail line and formed a sizeable Ashkenazi community complete with Jewish hospitals, synagogues, restaurants and fur shops. The last group of Jewish immigrants to arrive in the city were German, Austrian and Polish refugees. Unfortunately, their arrival coincided with that of the Japanese. During World War II, these 'stateless refugees' were ordered into a two square-kilometre 'designated area' in Hongkou district, known as the Shanghai Jewish Ghetto.

The stone tablet at the entrance to Huoshan Park is Shanghai's only public monument to the area's historic role as a Jewish safe-haven. From the park, walk down Zhoushan Road to Changyang Road, once the main street of the ghetto. There are still a few plaques and symbolic details remaining on house walls and down narrow alleys. Still standing at number 62 is the **Ohel Moshe Synagogue**, founded by Russian Jews in 1927. The small **Jewish Refugees Museum** on the third floor serves as a memorial to the refugees and their ties to Shanghai.

For a deeper insight into Shanghai's Jewish history, Israeli documentarian Dvir Bar-Gal hosts minutely-researched walking tours held daily in English or Hebrew (www.shanghai-jews.com).

*Shanghai Jewish Refugees Museum; 62 Changyang Road; tel: 6512 6669; daily 9am–5pm; charge; map E6*

# Step into 1933, a former abattoir and Art Deco masterpiece

Art Deco is Shanghai's signature style: the streamlined elegant look, born at the Exposition for the Decorative Arts in Paris in 1925, was a metaphor for the new age of skyscrapers, steamships, trains and all things *moderne*. Progressive Shanghai embraced it eagerly, but made it her own by adding Chinese elements.

Art Deco defined the city skyline between the late 1920s and '40s, and permeated virtually all design, industrial buildings included. Built in 1933, the old Shanghai Abattoir became Asia's most prolific slaughterhouse. The sloping concrete bridges criss-crossing the conical interior were noted not just as supremely functional for the mass transportation of cattle, but also as an era-defining example of industrial design. Sat imperiously beside a meandering creek, with its geometrically precise Art Deco lines, squares and portholes, the imposing stone exterior of the building deliberately suggested a Bund-front municipal office, bank or cultural centre, rather than a meat-processing plant.

After ceasing meatpacking operations, the building was converted into a medicine factory in 1970 before later falling into disrepair. The new century brought a local government-commissioned restoration of the abattoir and a handful of adjacent structures. Reopened in 2007 as a 'creative lifestyle hub', the renamed 1933 development has not really found its feet – partially due to bad management and an out-of-centre location. A handful of shops and restaurants occupy its varied spaces, but a visit to witness this fine piece of industrial art – especially the restored roundhouse upper level, which is used as a creative events space – is more than merited.

*1933; 10 Shajing Road; www.1933 shanghai.com; map E4*

# Take a shine to the Shanghai Museum of Glass

Located in the dramatically restyled Shanghai Glass Factory in the northern manufacturing district of Baoshan, the Shanghai Museum of Glass, which opened in 2011, is one of China's most original modern museums.

Glass is a predominant element in Shanghai's 21st-century skyline. This, plus the city's role as China's high-tech glass hub, was the inspiration for the Shanghai Glass Company to commission a museum outlining the contrasting timelines of glass technology and arts in Asia and the West. Designed in spacy black with copious glass panelling and colourful reflective lighting, it takes visitors on a superbly curated journey from ancient Egypt through the Middle Ages and China's Tang and Song dynasties to 21st-century glass applications used in China's space programme.

Video clips and installations showcase the role of glass design and technology in everything from the *24* television series to Barack Obama's Presidential acceptance speech, and the seabed dredging of crystal treasures from the Titanic.

The highlight of the museum is its collection of glass art and sculpture from around the world displayed on the third floor balcony. From Baccarat's *Nuclear Pomegranate* to Mossi vases inspired by Lalique and Chinese artist Shan Shan Sheng's Bamboo Forest installation, which was created from hand-blown Murano glass from Italy, this is real crystalline class.

*685 Changning Road West; tel: 6618 1970; www.shmog.org; Tue–Sun 9.30am– 4.30pm, until 9pm on Sat; map D8*

# Seek out cutting-edge Chinese art at the funky warehouse galleries of M50

Over the last decade or so, the clusters of deserted mills along Suzhou Creek have become a fertile breeding ground for Shanghai's contemporary art community. Artists and bohemian types flocked to this once-seedy neighbourhood, attracted to the large, bright factory and warehouse spaces – and low rents.

The largest of these artists' enclaves is M50, a funky catch-all name given to the collection of galleries in the former Xinhe Cotton Mill, at 50 Moganshan Road. M50 is the hub of the Chinese contemporary art boom in Shanghai, and is home to hundreds of artists' studios and professional galleries. Just a few years ago, these Concession-era warehouses were dilapidated spaces. Today they have been reinvented and many of the galleries – and the artists – have taken on a sophisticated veneer that can only come from selling expensive art.

A stroll through the galleries, which carry everything from well-known artists to emerging talents,

## Shanghart Taopu

Shanghai's art community is now venturing even further afield in pursuit of afforda-ble and intriguing gallery space. One of the latest enclaves to emerge is Shanghart Taopu. Billed as a warehouse style art museum, the unmissable zig-zag shaped red building offers a bright showroom exhibiting large installation and sculptural works, a café selling art books and products, plus an original archival room of Chinese contemporary art. Surrounding the gallery are several artist's workshops. Act like a collector and you may be allowed to poke your head in and meet the creators.

*18 Wuwei Road; tel: 3632 2097; Wed–Sun 10am–6pm; map D6*

photography to installation, takes you on a tour of Chinese contem-porary art – featuring both the commercial and the cutting edge. Many of the galleries are closed on Mondays.

Excellent galleries to look out for include Italian-Chinese **Aike Gallery** (Room 102, Building 0; tel: 5252 0010; www.dearco.it), which has a sister gallery in Palermo and **Vanguard Gallery** (A204, Building 4; www.vanguardgallery.com) which focuses on the new works of emerging artists.

Two of M50's pioneering gal-leries are also still going strong. Initiated in Shanghai in 1996, **ShanghART** (Building 16; tel: 6359 3923; www.shanghartgallery.com) has become one of the country's most influential art institutions and has taken a lead in representing Chinese artists on the interna-tional stage. Its soaring gallery is complemented by the neighbour-ing **H Space**, which hosts large installations and exhibitions.

Also commanding a sprawl-ing warehouse space, **Eastlink** (5/F, Building 6; tel: 6276 9932; www.eastlinkgallery.cn) champi-ons the work of China's innovative experimental artists.

For those interested in photo-graphic art, **Ofoto Gallery** (www.ofoto-gallery.com) presents cutting-edge photography in a sprawling series of rooms beneath an exposed loft ceiling.

Further down the road at 97 Mo-ganshan Road, **M97** (tel: 6266 1597; www.m97gallery.com) is another exciting venue for art photography enthusiasts.

*M50; 50 Moganshan Road; most galleries open Tue-Sun 10am-6pm; map D6*

# Saunter across Waibaidu Bridge and between the landmark buildings at its northern end

Cross into Hongkou the old-fashioned way, over **Waibaidu Bridge**, which spans the Suzhou Creek – and much of the neighbourhood's history. When it was completed in 1908, the bridge (known then by the English as Garden Bridge) was only expected to last 40 years. More than a century later, it still carries traffic across Suzhou Creek to Hongkou district, where the late 19th-century American settlement was located.

Built at the confluence of Suzhou Creek and the Huangpu River, China's first steel bridge replaced earlier wooden bridges and allowed the International Settlement along the Bund to expand northwards.

During the Japanese Occupation, the bridge served as the demarcation line between occupied Hongkou and the International Settlement; it was guarded by turbaned Sikh policemen from the British forces on the Bund side and Japanese soldiers on the occupied side.

In 2009, a century after its construction, the entire bridge was floated to a downstream workshop for restoration and reinforcement to ensure that it can continue to carry motor and pedestrian traffic for decades to come. Today, the bridge is a great vantage point for views of Pudong to the east and the Suzhou Creek to the west.

**Suzhou Creek: north bank**

The Victorian building at the northern end of Waibaidu Bridge is the **Astor House Hotel** – once one of Shanghai's most elegant hotels. Opened in 1911, it attracted the illustrious likes of Charlie Chaplin and Albert Einstein. The hotel is a little less exclusive these days, but the interior has largely been spared modernisation making a wander across creaky antique teak floors and through the high-ceilinged corridors hung with sepia photos of famous guests, particularly enchanting. On the third floor, the vaulted Tudor-style hall holds a mini museum of hotel artefacts.

Sat beside the water's edge next to Astor House is the **Russian Consulate**. Dating back to 1916, it appears from the river like a luxury Soviet-era dacha. Today, the Russian Federation is the only country still occupying its original Shanghai consulate building.

Diagonally opposite, the cigar-coloured **Broadway Mansions** looms large. The 19-storey building was built as a luxury serviced apartment block in 1934, its bold Art Deco form taking in the full panorama of the Bund. It is best remembered as the wartime Foreign Correspondents Club, which occupied the top six floors. Since 1951 it has operated as a state-run hotel – and little of the period interior has survived.

Continue along Suzhou Creek, beyond the imposing **Shanghai Post Office** (see page 145) to the **Embankment Building**, designed by prolific architects Palmer & Turner for Victor Sassoon in 1932. The streamlined dove-grey Art Deco complex was the largest apartment building in the Far East, with wide balconies, eight elevators, and servants' quarters for most apartments. It even had its own artesian well providing fresh water for the residents and a heated swimming pool.

Today, several of the huge apartments have been wonderfully restored. At **Chai Living** (www.chai living.com), you can book a short stay in one of these artistically renovated apartments with superb city views. Spanish tapas and cocktails are served at **Chai Living Lounge & Gallery** (370 Suzhou North Road; tel: 3603 3511) downstairs.

*Astor House Hotel; 15 Huangpu Road; tel: 6324 6388; map D2*
*Broadway Mansions; 20 Suzhou North Road; map D2*
*Embankment Building; 400 Suzhou North Road; map C2*

# Discover the secrets of Chiang Kai-shek's 'new city', a fusion of Art Deco and Ming-dynasty design

During the 1930s, China's ruling Kuomintang Nationalist government devised a 'grand plan' to build a 'new Shanghai' civic centre in the northern Jiangwan district, far removed from the city's foreign concessions. When Chiang Kai-shek's Nationalists were defeated by Mao's Communists in 1949, the grandiose 'new city' plan was abandoned. The buildings that remain are classic examples of the fusion of Art Deco and Ming Chinese styles, and worth a detour.

A short walk from Xiangyin Road metro station (Line 8, Exit 4), what was built in 1935 as the Shanghai Museum is Building 10 of the **Changhai Hospital**. The museum's grand central hall is a patient waiting room, but you can wander in to glimpse the original paintwork and mosaics. Close by, Building 12 is the former Aviation Society Building,

designed in the shape of an Art Deco-styled aeroplane. Opposite the hospital, in the campus grounds of the **Shanghai University of Sport**, is the former City Hall. The impressive palace-like structure is now a campus administrative building, but visitors are permitted to explore the brightly decorated corridors.

One structure still used for its original purpose is Jiangwan Stadium. It was the largest in east Asia when it was completed in 1935 with a capacity of 40,000. Jiangwan Stadium metro station (Line 10) is a short walk from here.

*Changhai Hospital; 168 Changhai Road; map E7*
*Shanghai University of Sport; 345 Changhai Road; map E7*
*Jiangwan Stadium; 346 Guohe Road; tel: 5522 4216; map E7*

# Stock up on textiles and tuck in to lamb kebabs at the Friday Muslim Market

Stroll along Changde Road on a Friday afternoon and it's hard to believe you're in Shanghai. The aroma of paprika lamb kebabs fills the air and women in traditional dress sell dried fruit as men in white skull-caps emerge from the Huxi Mosque. Naan breads are lined up on carts ready to be devoured, and carpets hang from makeshift stands. This part of town is a haven for Shanghai's Muslims, most of whom come from the Uighur ethnic community. More Turkic than Han, the Uighur people hail from Xinjiang Province in China's far west. Of China's 55 ethnic minorities, 10 are variants of the Muslim faith, but all worship side by side at the Huxi Mosque.

Every Friday at around 11am, vendors begin to set up shop along a single block of Changde Road opposite the mosque. When prayers finish at 1pm, the market bustles with life. Get there at around midday to soak up the atmosphere, and snag the best mutton kebabs and pumpkin dumplings hot off the grill. Xinjiang Province is famous for its lamb dishes, especially *yangrou chuan* skewers, made with juicy chunks of mutton interspersed with fat from the tail. These cost just a handful of yuan each, and go well with naan bread and an iced yoghurt drink.

The market has been bustling for around six years, but the first Huxi Mosque dates to 1914 when Muslims from rural provinces arrived in Shanghai. The current mosque was built in 1992 and has a two-storey prayer hall. The Friday market is a linchpin of the city's Muslim community, and a chance for Uighur people to dress in their traditional costume, meet up with friends and sell the wares of their home province.

*Muslim Market; Corner of Changde Road and Aomen Road; Fri 11am–mid-afternoon; map D6*

# Explore the meandering Suzhou Creek and visit a Chocolate Factory

Shanghai's secondary waterway, **Suzhou Creek** (also known as Wusong River) runs 125km (78 miles) inland from the Huangpu River to Lake Tai. Historically, it was a commercial barge route for transporting goods from the Shanghai docks to neighbouring cities. During the booming 1930s, warehouses, factories and glamorous residences sprang up along its meandering banks. By the end of the century, however, the water was heavily polluted and the area badly neglected. A multi-million dollar clean-up operation was launched in the mid-1990s to restore Suzhou Creek as a place to live and work. Art galleries and studios began occupying old warehouses, trendy office spaces and event venues were created in derelict factories, and high-rise apartments emerged to the detriment of several historic neighbourhoods that were razed.

Today, Suzhou Creek merits a visit to see how this industrial hinterland has been re-landscaped as part of Shanghai's greater urban plan. Some fine examples of 1930s residential and industrial architecture reside along both banks. As you head inland, don't forget to look back – the views of Pudong from 'The Creek' are superb.

A short taxi ride away in Hongkou district, **Zotter Chocolate Theatre** let's you realise your Willy Wonka fantasies. The Austrian chocolatier produces exquisite organic, fairtrade chocolate in 365 creative flavours (cheese chocolate, anyone?). The huge Shanghai atelier – the first outside Austria, housed in a heritage cotton storage warehouse – takes visitors on an endorphin-fuelled journey through their 'bean to bar' production processes. Tempting tastings of the fine-quality chocolate en route are part of the experience. You can even create your own flavours at the Mi-Xing Bar. Great fun for all ages.

*Zotter Chocolate Theatre; Shanghai International Fashion Centre, Building 9, 2866 Yanshupu Road; Tue–Fri 11am–6pm, Sat–Sun 10am–7pm; www.zotter.cn*

# Blow your mind and tastebuds at an exclusive 10-seat molecular restaurant

Set in a secret location beside Suzhou Creek, experimental eatery **Ultraviolet** is the brainchild of university chemistry major turned culinary inventor, Paul Pairet, the creative force behind the popular brasserie Mr & Mrs Bund (see page 34). Ultraviolet is the French chef's dream project, designed to broaden the parameters of a restaurant meal and rethink the way our senses interact when we eat.

Pairet does this with a 20-course set menu, whereby each staged course is accompanied by a 'choreographed interplay of sensory components' – from projections and scent to music and mists. Catering to just 10 patrons a night, the high-tech dining room is wired with a light projection tracking system with infrared cameras able to follow plates around the table, a dry scent diffuser wafting Givaudan aromas, and a panoramic screen showing immersive projections, from seascapes to 1950s wallpaper.

Imagine a gothic rock n' roll church scene with the faint scent of cathedral stone, AC/DC's Hells Bells blasting and a nitro-frozen palate cleanser of apple wasabi that melts so fast it's served directly in the mouth – communion style. Other dishes that may feature on any given night include 'Encapsulated Bouillabaisse', a single Cuttlefish Noodle presented in a concentric circle, and Tomato Peach 'No Shark Fin' Soup – each presented with their own mind- and palate-bending scenarios. Expect to be wowed.

*Ultraviolet; www.uvbypp.cc*

# Take a dip in a sky-high Jacuzzi and sip alfresco martinis at Vue Bar

Sited on the bend of the Huangpu River on the North Bund, atop the luxury Hyatt hotel (shanghai.grand.hyatt.com), **Vue** boasts a truly unique vista – staring straight down Shanghai's main artery, flanked to the right by the classical architecture of the Bund and to the left by the glassy futurism of Pudong. Spectacular by day, the panorama is truly sensational at night – especially from the rooftop Jacuzzi.

Vue is a multi-concept penthouse venue comprising a modern European restaurant designed like a private residence on the 30th floor of the Hyatt's West Tower, plus six private dining rooms on the 31st floor. The lounge action begins on the 32nd floor in Vue Bar. Styled by Japan's in-demand Super Potato interior design team, it features a wine cellar style entrance, exposed brick walls, fibre glass partitions and a circular bar surrounded by floor-to-ceiling glass to optimise the view.

So far, so cool, but ascend a sweeping staircase to the 33rd floor for the *pièce de résistance*. The stairway opens out onto a roofless deck terrace offering comfy day-beds, a resident DJ – and a circular Jacuzzi for sipping Vue-tini cocktails and sightseeing in sync. The stunning views and breezy deck make this a hot Sunday afternoon spot for post-brunch lounging. In the evenings, Shanghai's beautiful people sip and splash as the city around them dazzles in neon. And don't worry if you have forgotten your swimming gear – 'Vue Jacuzzi Wear' can be ordered from the bar menu.

*Hyatt on the Bund; 199 Huangpu Road; tel: 6393 1234 ext 6348 (lounge), ext 6328 (restaurant); www.shanghai.bund.hyatt.com; map E2*

# Come face to face with a Greek god atop Shanghai's Post Office tower

Occupying a prime site at the north end of the Sichuan Road Bridge on the banks of Suzhou Creek is the **Shanghai Post Office**. Built in 1924, it handled foreign mail for all 48 nationalities officially represented in Shanghai at the time, and is still the city's main post office today.

The stately stone building, encompassing an entire city block, is fronted by Corinthian columns and topped by a bronze capped Baroque bell tower. The interiors of the main postal hall are just as impressive, decorated with original black and white mosaic tiling, carved wooden service windows and handsomely coffered ceilings.

Pass through the operational postal hall to the newly renovated **Shanghai Post Museum** (Wed, Thur, Sat, Sun 9am–5pm; free) which charts the history of the Chinese postal system, from ancient beacon towers to modern mechanisation using interactive models, archival photographs and postal memorabilia.

When you've finished exploring the different exhibits (don't miss the precious stamp hall displaying postal stamp art across the decades), exit into the beautiful internal atrium courtyard and, if open, take the lift to the rooftop. The landscaped roof garden is the building's greatest asset, offering grassed-over areas, sensational views over Shanghai and a close-up look at the magnificent clock tower adorned with bronze statues of Greek gods Hermes, Eros and Aphrodite. Be sure to snap a photo from here of the futuristic Shanghai skyline, set against the classical stone urns along the roof ledge.

*Shanghai Post Office; 250 Suzhou Road North; daily 8am–10pm; tel: 6393 6666; map C2*

# XUHUI, CHANGNING AND HONGQIAO

# Xuhui, Changning and Hongqiao

E · F · G · H

5

Mokkos

ZHONGSHAN GONGYUAN
Toriyasu
ZHONGSHAN PARK

JIANGSU RD

Fu 1088

LOUSHANGUAN RD
Tianshan Tea City
Tentekomai

YAN'AN RD

Shanty

CHANGNING

Yan'an Road West

Shunxing

Hongqiao State Guesthouse

JIANTONG UNIVERSITY

The Door

HONGQIAO GONGYUAN

Redtown

ZHAOJIABANG RD

LUBAN RD

YULI RD
SONGYUAN RD

HONGQIAO RD

Soong Qingling's Mausoleum
Yamatoya

Hongsong Road

XUJIAHUI

Power Station of Art

Xujiahui Tianzhutang (St Ignatius Cathedral)

Bibliotheca Zikawei

DAMUQIAO RD

YISHAN RD

Pyongyang Okryu

DONGAN RD

Nanpu Railway Station

SHANGHAI STADIUM

XUHUI

MIDDLE LONGHUA RD

SHANGHAI INDOOR STADIUM

SHANGHAI SWIMMING CENTER

Long Museum

3

GUILIN RD

CAOXI RD

LONGHUA LIESHI LINGYUAN (LONGHUA MARTYRS MEMORIAL CEMETERY)

LONGHUA

Yishan Road

GUILIN GONGYUAN

Caobao Road

LONGCAO RD

YUNJIN RD

Fenggu Rd

Yuz Museum

Shanghai Centre of Photography

Huangpu

CAOBAO RD

2

SHILONG RD

LONGYAO RD

SHANGHAI SOUTH RAILWAY STATION

Shilong Road

Shanghai South Railway Station

Shanghai Zhiwuyuan (Botanical Garden)

JINJIANG PARK

Balse Road

Humin Road

Middle Ring Road

1

E · F · G · H

# Discover the best little izakayas and hidden shochu bars in Japan-town

In the 1990s, Japanese entrepreneurs poured into Shanghai, settling in the western suburbs. Two decades later, Hongqiao is a veritable Little Japan. Fukuoka ramen? Sumo wrestler hot pot? Fourth-generation tempura master? Shanghai has them all. None are as fun, however, as the *izakaya*, the uniquely Japanese blend of restaurant and pub.

You'll find **Toriyasu** (172 Huichuan Road; tel: 5241 1677; daily 5.30pm–1am; map E5) by its slatted-wood facade and sadistically small door. The menu comes hand-written in tiny Chinese characters (there's also a smaller translated English menu). No matter. Sit in front of the smoky charcoal grill, the source of Toriyasu's magic, and point to what's cooking: butterflied chicken wings, thighs threaded with fat leeks, tomatoes wrapped in bacon. Wash it down with draft Asahi or a flask of sake – and duck on the way out.

At **Tentekomai** (295 Wuyi Road; tel: 6212 9755; daily 5.30–11.30pm; map F5) a quaint *izakaya*, the door is normal-sized; it's the gyoza that is tiny. Snack on the one-bite dumplings before walking down the street to **Shanty** (84 Wuyi Road; tel: 6225 8635; daily 7.30pm–2am; map F5) the hush-hush *shochu* and plum bar of a resident Japanese trader. The Russian bartender, fluent in Japanese and English, will offer up suggestions, but to snag one of the 14 seats, you'll have to swallow the RMB50 sitting fee.

Heading back towards downtown, not far from Toriyasu, **Mokkos Lamu** (1245 Wuding West Road; tel: 6212 1114; daily 7pm–2am; map G5) is a secret Japanese bar tucked away down a dark alley. Pull open the unassuming wooden door to discover this friendly little drinking den that draws a mixed crowd to sip the bar specialty spirit, Japanese *shochu*. The hip young couple behind the sunken sit-up bar are happy to explain the different varieties, distilled from everything from barley and rice to sweet potato. They also shake some refreshing citrus-infused *shochu* cocktails. A reggae soundtrack and welcoming vibe make Mokkos Lamu a wonderfully chilled place to wind up a Japanese-themed evening.

# Stock up on tea leaves at Tianshan Tea City

For a mall dedicated solely to caffeinated products, Tianshan Tea City is a remarkably calm place. Perhaps it's the influence of the faux-temple architecture. The halls of this three-storey tea emporium are lined with little shops specialising in everything from high-elevation Taiwanese oolongs to Hangzhou's Dragon Well green.

Head to the first floor for a lesson in the surrounding region's green tea types, which are among the best in the country. Small plates display the tight curls of Suzhou's *biluochun*, the paddle-like *Taiping houkui* ('monkey-picked'), and the flat blades of Hangzhou's *longjing* (Dragon Well), China's most famous green tea. Stop, sit, sniff, sip, say thank you, and move on. There are two more floors to go.

From the parking lot, ascend the escalator at the yellow sign. Turn left and pop into Wuyi Star (No. 2093) for their signature Fujianese oolong, *da hongpao* ('big red robe'), in colour-coded tins (white for fragrance, gold for flavour). Around the next corner, past the Yixing clay teapots, are the oval leaves of Liu'an *guapian*, an unusual green said to resemble melon seeds (No. 2053).

Prefer milk and sugar? Stall 2008 specialises in Keemun, a fruity black that's a prime ingredient in English breakfast tea. Don't do that to the expensive oolongs at No. 2076 though, plucked from the top of Taiwan's highest mountains, or the pricey discs of aged *pu'erh*, a dark and smoky black from Yunnan that's the preserve of serious teaheads.

Casual drinkers should drop into Linzhiyu (No. 3028), a hip spot among the third floor's dusty curio stores, for the Hershey Kiss-sized *pu'erh* samples and, surprisingly, wild honey from the young couple's Yunnan hometown.

*Tianshan Tea City; 518 Zhongshan Road West; www.dabutong.com; daily 8.30am–8.30pm; map E5*

# Slip on a pair of tropical pyjamas and explore the kooky world of the Chinese bathhouse

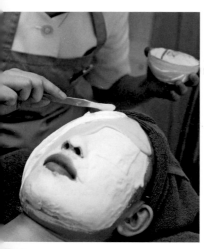

For the uninhibited, a Chinese bathhouse experience offers unforgettable cultural insights. A hangover from the days when most households didn't have showering facilities, a visit to the bathhouse remains popular. The modern-day variety has morphed into an all-in-one entertainment emporium, offering round-the-clock bathing (starting from RMB88), gaming, dining and more.

For good, clean family fun, try **Xiao Nan Guo Tang He Yuan** in Hongqiao. The bathhouse lobby resembles a retro five-star hotel, with chandeliers, a marble check-in counter and self-playing grand piano. Here the similarities end, because patrons of this five-storey pleasure palace pad around in garish Hawaiian mumus – or nothing at all.

Leave your shoes (and modesty) at reception and head into the segregated changing rooms and bathing areas filled with unclothed bodies. Signage is in Chinese but it's easy to pick out the milk, 'green' and Japanese baths. Between dips, there's a cold plunge pool, steam room and sauna. After your soak, head to the communal scrubbing room for a 30-minute all-over body exfoliation. A small extra fee earns you a facemask of cucumber pulp or a dousing in drinking milk.

After showering, it's time to towel off and pull on the regulation Hawaiian pyjamas to explore the rest of the emporium, where various rooms feature ping pong, snooker, mahjong and karaoke. If you're feeling hungry, multiple cafés serve restorative noodles and dim sum. Finish up at the huge foot massage area where reclining beds are fitted with mini TV screens. Save on a hotel and spend the night here if you wish!

*Xiao Nan Guo Tang He Yuan; 3337 Hongmei Road; tel: 6465 8888; daily 11am–9am; charge; map D4*

# Select premium pearls and design your own jewellery at Hongqiao Pearl City

There's no better place to shop for pearls than China, which overtook Japan as the world's number one supplier in 2010. As Shanghai is located near to the freshwater pearling areas of China, they're particularly cheap and, with some 30 or so vendors, **Hongqiao Pearl City** offers better choice and prices than elsewhere in the town.

Located in the Japanese and Korean quarter of Shanghai, the market is in a mall in a shopping district dotted with anime bookshops and *bibimbap* (mixed rice with vegetables) restaurants. The mall itself is a garish 1990s construction and the bottom floor houses a fake goods market. On the second floor, however, is a relatively crowd-free pearl market absent of the usual onslaught of hawkers.

Expect to bargain hard – first-quoted prices can be triple or quadruple what you should pay. A pair of freshwater pearl earrings should cost RMB20 and strings of pearls around RMB200, though the bigger the pearls and more perfectly rounded, the costlier. For timeless pearl studs, **Daxi Pearl** at the top of the escalator couples friendly, English-speaking service with a good selection. If you feel creative, **Vicky Pearl** at G050 is one of the best places to customise your own jewellery. Staff speak English, and you can choose the type of chain, setting, pearl shape and colour, though note: only white, black, pink, lavender and peach naturally occur.

It's relatively easy to tell if a pearl is genuine by simply looking at it, but vendors are happy to do a 'scrape test' – where they tease tiny shards off the back of a pearl with a knife – to prove they're not painted plastic. A smudge of the thumb smoothes any potential scratches.

*Hongqiao Pearl City; 3721 Hongmei Road; daily 10am–9pm; map D4*

# Explore the manicured gardens and ornamental lakes of Changning District's state guesthouses

While the metropolitan parks of the city centre can be less than relaxing (with crowds of people, loud music blaring, and odd rules governing where you can and can't venture), the beautiful state guesthouses of Changning District and their sprawling manicured grounds provide a more peaceful experience.

The **Hongqiao State Guesthouse** has one of the most beautiful green spaces in the city – a park that is rarely visited due to its somewhat hidden location. The five-star hotel is part of the state-owned Donghu Hotels group, and became an official lodging house when Deng Xiaoping decided to create state guesthouses in the 1980s to accommodate visiting dignitaries. What makes Hongqiao State Guesthouse particularly special is the 50-acre green space surrounding it. The gardens are part of the former country estate of Sir Victor Sassoon, the British-Jewish real estate tycoon whose inner-city residence was under the copper dome of his most famous property, the Peace Hotel.

The land retains the charm of days gone by, with paths winding through forests, bamboo groves and carpets of bluebells in spring, and ornamental stone chairs where visitors can sit and soak up the atmosphere.

Sassoon's legacy also lives on in the **Cypress Hotel**, 5km (3 miles) to the southwest. The property's original Tudor-style mansion now forms building No. 1 of the Jinjiang-owned guesthouse.

*Hongqiao State Guesthouse; 1591 Hongqiao Road; tel: 6219 8855; www.hq stateguesthotel.com; map E4*
*Cypress Hotel; 2419 Hongqiao Road; tel: 6322 3855; www.cypresshotelshanghai. cn; map C3*

# Paint the town at contemporary art and music enclave, Redtown

An old state-run steelworks to the west of the former French Concession is now an arts district, typifying the metamorphosis that spawned lifestyle hubs like Xintiandi and Tianzifang. Known as Redtown, the complex started life as the Shanghai No. 1 Steel Factory in 1956. Nowadays, the main factory building has been converted into a cavernous art space, while the surrounding lanes are home to cafés, bars, galleries, shops, creative businesses and random outdoor artworks. Most of the venues are closed on Mondays.

**Shanghai Sculpture Space** (tel: 6280 5629) opened in 2005, and dominates Redtown with its giant 10,000-sq-metre (108,000 sq ft) indoor area (split into Halls A and B) and sprawling garden. A mix of permanent and temporary displays keeps things fresh. If you need a caffeine fix after browsing the installations, head to nearby **Sculpting in Time Cafe** (Suite B111; 5258 8218). A contemporary bohemian vibe forms the backdrop for good coffee, teas, cakes and snacks.

Another large-scale venue for showcasing the work of contemporary Chinese artists is the **Minsheng Art Museum**. Founded by Minsheng Bank, the 4,000-sq-metre gallery is divided into five exhibition halls, and there's also an art bookshop.

Music lovers won't want to miss **BOTH Music and Boutique** (Suite B106). The funky raw-brick space stocks smart men's fashions, satchels, footwear and fixie bikes, but the Music Café is even cooler. More than 150 hip-hop, funk, soul, and rare groove vinyl are displayed on the walls. Borrow a personal turntable and headphones free of charge and listen to your favourite records over a beer or coffee. Thanks to its position on the outskirts of the old French Concession, Redtown is spared the crowds that turn Xintiandi and Tianzifang manic at weekends.

*Redtown; 570 Huaihai Road West; www.redtownsh.com; map F4*

# Discover contemporary art in a military aircraft hangar or power station along the West Bund Cultural Corridor

Following the Huangpu River south from the Bund, an 8.4km (5.2 mile) stretch of industrial port area has been redeveloped as a waterfront arts district. Dubbed the West Bund Cultural Corridor, it is home to several private museums in inspiring warehouse spaces.

**Long Museum** was founded by Chinese billionaire couple collectors Liu Yiqian and Wang Wei. The bold industrial space hosts regularly rotating exhibitions of Chinese contemporary art alongside an arresting array of revolutionary art and antiquities.

Nearby, **Yuz Museum** occupies a former military aircraft hangar. The soaring 9,000-sq-metre gallery showcases works from Chinese-Indonesian tycoon Budi Tek's huge contemporary art collection plus blockbuster exhibits like a forthcoming collaboration with Paris' Picasso Museum in 2017.

**More modern art**
Close to the waterfront between the West Bund and Old Town, the excellent **Power Station of Art**, China's first state-run contemporary art museum, has transformed a heritage riverside power plant with a towering smokestack that lights up like a thermometer. It now hosts the Shanghai Biennale.

*200 Huayuangang Road; tel: 3110 8550; www.powerstationofart.org/en; Tue-Sun 11am-7pm*

**Shanghai Centre of Photography** is a bright, airy gallery-museum showcasing contemporary and archival photography shot in China and across the globe.

Coming in 2017 to this ever-evolving area is DreamWorks' $2.5 billion **Shanghai DreamCentre**, featuring an animation studio, IMAX theatre and Legoland Discovery Centre, along with restaurants.

*Long Museum, 3398 Longteng Avenue; tel: 6422 7636; www.thelongmuseum.org; Tue-Sun 10am-6pm, last entry 5pm; map H3*
*Yuz Museum; 35 Fenggu Road; tel: 6210 5207; daily 10.30am-5.30pm; map H2*
*Shanghai Centre of Photography; 2555 Longteng Avenue; Tues-Sun 10.30am-5.30pm; map H2*

# Eat with the elite in a colonial villa setting at Fu 1088 and Fu He Hui

Only the doormen mark out this colonial villa as a restaurant. Originally a residence of a powerful relative (whispered to be a Kuomintang general), the elegant mansion passed through owner Fu Yafen's family and managed to survive Shanghai's tumultuous history almost fully intact; the gorgeous Spanish tile and cherry-wood staircases are original and antiques fill the 17 rooms, where the film-set atmosphere meets chef Tony Lu's refined Shanghainese cooking.

*Xunyu* has emerged as Lu's calling card. Warm, fragrant, and the colour of dark mahogany, **Fu 1088**'s version is a stack of river fish marinated in soy sauce, sugar, and rice wine before a light frying. He does as well with *hongshao rou*, succulent and melting red-braised pork belly, and cold 'drunken chicken', a speciality of nearby Shaoxing that uses that city's well-known rice wine as a marinade.

Shanghai's surrounds are crisscrossed by lakes and rivers, and it's from these waterways that the city's cuisine is drawn: 'crystal' river shrimp, sautéed with the leaves of Hangzhou's famous *long-jing* tea, or a Reeves shad steamed in yellow rice wine and the region's Jinhua ham. It's worth noting that

there is a minimum RMB400 spend per person.

Tony Lu – Shanghai's most celebrated local chef – has opened a Buddhist vegetarian restaurant, **Fu He Hui**, down the road. Serving exquisite prix fixe menus, it was voted as one of Asia's 50 Best Restaurants in 2016.

*Fu 1088, 375 Zhenning Road; tel: 5239 7878; daily 11am–2pm, 5.30–11pm; map F5*
*Fu He Hui, 1037 Yuyuan Road; tel: 3980 9188; map F5*

# Take a warp-speed trip on one of China's amazing 'bullet' trains

The ongoing expansion of airports and high-speed railways is transforming domestic travel in China. At the beginning of 2016, China had 19,000 km (12,000 miles) of high-speed track in operation, with plans for this total to be 30,000 km (19,000 mi) by 2020.

Shanghai is leading the way for transport infrastructure upgrading. Its second airport, Hongqiao, welcomed a large new terminal in 2010, and was joined by a new railway station (map A4) for super-fast travel around China. Both the airport and rail station are easily accessed using Metro Line 2 or 10 from downtown.

Travelling at up to 390km/h (243mph), China's 'bullet' trains have slashed journey times, making excursions from Shanghai ever more appealing. The Unesco World Heritage-listed classical gardens of Suzhou are now just a 30-minute train ride away, and the mystical West Lake and tea plantations of Hangzhou take 50 minutes to reach. There's even a high-speed train service linking Shanghai and the capital, Beijing – the 1,318km (819-mile) ride on a bullet train takes just 4 hours and 48 minutes.

Expansion plans include a proposed extension of the MagLev train to connect Pudong and Hongqiao airports. The Hongqiao Commercial Hub, currently under construction and due to feature a 420-room 'urban resort' hotel, luxury brand mall, fine Asian dining and a space-age performing arts centre, will be directly linked to Hongqiao airport and rail station.

# Pay your respects to early Communist martyrs at one of Shanghai's most compelling monuments

Shanghai's revolutionary history is often packaged in hard-hitting state-speak that is heavy on rhetoric but less attentive to historic detail. The **Longhua Martyrs Memorial** Cemetery, while not short on pro-Communist hype, is a poignant reminder that amid the wordy political ideology, China's 20th-century social upheavals involved significant human pain and suffering.

The cemetery commemorates a tragic moment in Shanghai's history when hundreds of young Communists were killed during the Kuomintang's reign of terror. On 12 April 1927, these revolutionaries were rounded up and taken to the execution grounds in what was then the Longhua Garrison. Each April, Longhua's orchard of peach trees blossoms in remembrance.

The cemetery today is all meticulously landscaped gardens and high-tech fountains, with a blue-glass Louvre-esque pyramid and a Memorial Hall dedicated to the Communist martyrs. Outside an eternal flame burns in front of the *Tomb of the Unknown Martyrs*, sculpted by He Pan, which features a Herculean sculpture half-entombed in the lawn with an arm extending upward in hope. Dotted across the park other giant concrete socialist-realist statues depicting heroic revolutionary struggles against anti-Communist adversaries.

The Martyrs' Cemetery also features reconstructions of the Kuomintang prison and execution grounds, and a memorial museum that narrates (in English and Chinese) with images, videos and historical artefacts, the bloody revolutionary struggle after the founding of the Chinese Communist Party in 1921.

*Longhua Martyrs Memorial Cemetery; Longhua Road West; daily 7am–4.30pm; free; map G3*

# Pair a folk opera stage show with a fiery Sichuan feast

**Shunxing** is a grand old teahouse chain from Chengdu, the capital of southwest China's Sichuan province. This bastion of laconic Sichuan culture recently arrived in China's most harried city. This being Shanghai, the colourful traditional wooden gateway is tacked on to an office tower, but what lies within is pure Sichuan.

The action in this elegant 1,000-seat restaurant – each one a hefty, carved wooden chair – is centered on a classic Sichuanese opera stage, and just edges out the kitchen's own deft performance. Every night at 7.30pm, the resident troupe upbraids each other in sing-song dialect, wails through a repertoire of countryside opera, and performs a mesmerising 'face-changing' routine with an endless cache of silk masks.

Sichuan's other art, of course, is the region's famously fiery food, exemplified by Shunxing's outstanding rendition of *mapo doufu*, silky cubes of tofu in a glistening red bath of chillies and numbing Sichuan peppercorns.

For a more genteel evening in Old Shanghai, head to **The Door.** On weeknights from 6.30–8pm, quiet young ladies play traditional Chinese instruments like the *erhu* and *pipa* in the former military warehouse, now done up in high 1920s style. The nostalgic, pre-war touch extends beyond the antique furniture to the waiters in long tunics, who glide over the parquet floor bearing classic Shanghainese and Cantonese dishes.

*Shunxing; 2–3/F, 1088 Yan'an Road West; tel: 6213 8988; daily 11.30am–9.30pm, reserve for a stage-side table; map F4*
*The Door; 1468 Hongqiao Road; tel: 6295 1717; daily 10.45am–2pm, 4–11.30pm; map E4*

# Take a look inside Xujiahui Cathedral and browse the atmospheric Bibliotheca Zikawei

Today, the bustling Xujiahui district houses cathedrals of commerce, but a century ago this part of Shanghai was deeply Catholic territory. In fact, Xujiahui is named after the Xu family, whose descendent, Paul Xu (born 1562), was the first Chinese high official to convert to Christianity. He bequeathed his estate to French Jesuits who, in 1847, built a monastic complex which included a seminary, orphanage, workshops, printing press, Latin library and weather observation station.

The centrepiece of the complex is China's largest Catholic church. Completed in 1906, **St Ignatius Cathedral** (Xujiahui Cathedral) is a dramatic vision of red brick, stained glass and towering spires, both toppled during the Cultural Revolution when the cathedral was used as a grain store. Since then, the entire church has been restored and is once again used by the Catholic community. Take a peek inside the angel-white interiors and note the new stained glass panels, crafted by local nuns, incorporating modern Chinese symbolism and characters to illustrate the gospel stories.

The former priests' residence now houses the lovely **Bibliotheca Zikawei**, an incredible collection of rare books. The ground floor is designed in the style of a classic Qing library, while the beautiful upper floor is a fine copy of the Vatican Library. Breezy Italianate corridors, dark wood staircases and an atmospheric reading room make for delightful browsing.

*St Ignatius Cathedral; 158 Puxi Road; tel: 6438 2595; open for public viewing Sat–Sun 1–4.30pm; map F4*
*Bibliotheca Zikawei; 80 Caoxi Road North; tel: 6487 4095; free 15-min library tours on Sat 2–4pm; map F4*

# Unwind in the serene retreat of Guilin Park

In a high-density city like Shanghai, public parks and gardens provide welcome havens of solitude, space and social interaction. Chinese horticulturalists have long been experts at cultivating gorgeous Zen gardens. One of Shanghai's finest is **Guilin Park**. This charming walled garden was once the private residence of a not-so charming character – Huang Jingrong, or 'Pockmarked Huang', a notorious gangster who doubled up as head of police in the French Concession. The home and garden was completed over four years in the early 1930s.

Pay the RMB2 entrance fee to access this popular park landscaped with pagodas, grottoes, rockeries and century-old cypress and pine trees. The outer and inner

### Shanghai Botanical Garden
Not far from Guilin Park is the **Shanghai Botanical Garden**, an 80-hectare collection of multiple species of magnolias, peonies, azaleas, Chinese orchids, rhododendron, bamboo, maples and more.

*1111 Longwu Road; tel: 5436 3369; www.shbg.org; map G1*

gardens are separated by an undulating stone wall that was designed to resemble a dragon's back.

If you visit around September you are in for a special treat. The name Guilun Park refers to the more than 1,000 sweet *gui* (osmanthus) trees planted throughout. When the tiny cream flowers bloom at the first signs of autumn, the whole park is draped with an intoxicating fragrance.

The central Four Religion Hall is now a rustic teahouse. Pick your leaves and you'll be supplied with a large thermos of hot water. While away the afternoon on the ornately carved verandah sipping tea and watching senior citizens practice opera in the gardens and couples posing for Western-style pre-wedding pictures.

*Guilin Park; 128 Guilin Road; map E2*

# Visit the final resting place of Soong Qingling, one of China's most powerful women

The story of the three Soong sisters is one of the most compelling in modern Chinese history, and this peaceful park is a great place to learn about their lives while escaping the noise and bustle of central Shanghai. The **Mausoleum of Soong Qingling** contains a foreign cemetery, a museum, lush parkland and a children's activity area plus the final resting place of Qingling and her parents.

Soong Qingling (1893–1981) was one of the most powerful women in Chinese history, ruling the country alongside her husband, Dr Sun Yat-sen. Out of the three sisters, Qingling is remembered for her love of power. The eldest, Ailing, married Guomindang finance minister and millionaire H.H. Kung, garnering her a reputation for loving money. The youngest, Meiling, was the wife of Kuomintang leader Chiang Kai-shek, and is noted for her dedication to her country. The charismatic Soong Qingling, the only one of the influential Soong sisters to remain in China, is commemorated at this tranquil site in Shanghai's Changning district.

The Soong family plot is part of the Wan Guo cemetery that is also the resting place of patriots, war heroes and over 600 foreigners

from 25 countries. The centrepiece is Qingling's gravesite, with a white marble statue in her likeness. To the left is the final resting place of Lin Yan'e, Qingling's nanny and lifelong friend.

The **Soong Qingling Exhibition Hall** contains over 500 photographs and artefacts that offer insights into China's political and social history during the most turbulent periods of the 20th century.

*Soong Qingling's Mausoleum; 21 Songyuan Road; tel: 6474 7183; daily 8.30am–5pm; map E4*

# ESSENTIALS

## A

### ADDRESSES

In most modern buildings, the ground floor is 1/F. Buildings are sequentially numbered, odd numbers on one side of the street and even numbers on the other. Because the major streets often run the entire length of the city, it helps to know what the nearest cross-street is when trying to locate an address, such as Nanjing West Road near *(kaojing)* Maoming Road.

## B

### BUSINESS CARDS

In business and other formal situations in Shanghai, you will be expected to present a business card. Present cards with both hands, and accept them the same way to follow correct protocol.

## C

### CHILDREN

The Shanghainese adore children. There is not a museum, a restaurant or a theatre where your child will feel unwelcome. Hotels often allow children to stay with parents in a double room at no extra charge. Extra beds are available for a small surcharge. Reliable babysitters, known as *ayi* (aunty), are easily available.

### CLIMATE

Shanghai has a northern sub-tropical monsoon climate with four distinct seasons. Rainfall is plentiful throughout the year, though most of it falls during the rainy season from June to September.

Expect hot and muggy summers with temperatures hovering in the mid-30s°C (95°F) in July and August, and chilled-to-the-bone damp winters in December and January. January is the coldest month, although temperatures rarely dip below zero. Snow is rare in Shanghai, although there are the occasional late December/January flurries.

Shanghai's mildest weather (and correspondingly the best time to visit) is in spring (mid-March to May) and autumn (September to early November).

### CLOTHING

Shanghai errs on the side of casual, but it is a city of unrelenting style: you'll be forgiven for not wearing a tie, but never for looking like a bumpkin. Light, breathable clothes work best in the hot, humid summertime, with a light wrap for the over-air-conditioned restaurants and offices. In winter, several layers of clothing is the key to staying warm, as buildings are sometimes under-heated. Shanghai's evening dress code is increasingly hip and well groomed.

## CONSULATES

**Australian Consulate**: 22/F, CITIC Square, 1168 Nanjing Road West; tel: 5292 5500; www.china.embassy. gov.au

**British Consulate**: Suite 301, Shanghai Centre, 1376 Nanjing Road West; tel: 6279 7650; www.uk.cn

**New Zealand Consulate**: 1605–1607A, 989 Changle Road; tel: 5407 5858; www.nzembassy.com

**Singapore Consulate**: 89 Wanshan Road; tel: 6278 5566; www.mfa.gov. sg/shanghai

**United States Consulate**: 1469 Huaihai Middle Road; tel: 6433 6880; also American Citizen Services: 8/F, Westgate Mall, 1038 Nanjing Road West; tel: 3217 4650, after-hours emergencies tel: 6433 3936; http://shanghai.usconsulate.gov.

## CRIME AND SAFETY

Shanghai is a relatively safe city, but petty crimes like pickpocketing do occur in crowded areas like train stations, markets and on busy streets. There is very little violent crime against foreigners, but tourists should be aware of scams. It's a safe city for women, too, who are able to walk alone, even at night, without being harassed – but again, you should be on your guard.

## CUSTOMS

Duty-free allowance per adult is as follows: two bottles of liquor (75cl each) and 400 cigarettes. There is no limit to the amount of foreign currency and Chinese renminbi (RMB) traveller's cheques that can be brought in; the unspent portion may be taken out. There is a long list of prohibited items, including animals, firearms, plant material and media deemed 'detrimental' to China's social and political security. For up-to-date details see www.china.org.cn. Note: antiques require a government stamp in order to be exported; most reputable dealers can take care of the necessary paperwork.

## D

## DISABLED TRAVELLERS

Most of Shanghai's modern hotels, buildings and museums are all wheelchair-accessible, but older buildings and the myriad overpasses and underpasses are not. Newer metro stations all have wheelchair ramps or lifts, and the older ones are adding them. Bashi Taxi (tel: 6431 2788) has several minivans that cater for the wheelchair-bound.

## E

## ELECTRICITY

Shanghai's electrical system runs at 200/220 volts and 50 cycles AC. Sockets take Australian-style three-pin triangular plugs or circular two-pins. Chinese-to-foreign conversion accessories – whether conversion plugs or voltage converters – are easily available at department stores and hotels.

## EMERGENCY NUMBERS

Public Security Bureau: 710 Hankou Road; tel: 6321 5380

Ambulance: 120
Fire: 119
Police: 110

## F

## FURTHER READING

*Rise of a Hungry Nation: China Shakes the World*, James Kynge (2006). This excellent book by a former *Financial Times* Beijing bureau chief explains all you ever needed to know about the factors behind, and social consequences of, China's economic rise.

*New Shanghai Cuisine* (2005), Jereme Leung. Executive chef at the Whampoa Club takes a historical, and beautifully photographed, journey through the complex cuisine of Shanghai.

*Life & Death in Shanghai*, Nien Cheng (1987). Harrowing autobiographical tale, written in exile, about incarceration and survival during the Cultural Revolution;

*Western Architecture in Shanghai: A Last Look*, Tess Johnston and Deke Erh (2004). Beautifully photographed book chronicling the origins and architects of Shanghai's rich portfolio of western-influenced villas, mansions and historic houses.

*Carl Crow – A Tough Old China Hand*, Paul French (2006). Fascinating story of an intriguing character – an American journalist, ad-man and social networker – who became an intrinsic feature of 1920s/1930s Shanghai.

*In Search of Old Shanghai*, Lynn Pan (1982). Historical musings about old Shanghai by probably the city's best chronicler.

*Empire of the Sun* (1984), JG Ballard. This emotive wartime story of a young boy interned by the occupying Japanese would later became a major movie.

*The Where's Where of the Who's Who of Old Shanghai*, Tess Johnston (2016). The final edition of a much-loved walking guide series uncovers the colourful characters who once lived, loved and worked in Shanghai's historic buildings.

## H

## HEALTH

No vaccinations are required to enter Shanghai, but doctors often recommend immunisations against flu, tetanus and Hepatitis A & B. Tap water should be boiled before drinking and bottled water is widely available. For current information on influenza and other health concerns, see www.who.int/csr/en.

### Medical services

Healthcare is good in Shanghai, and improving all the time. There are Western-staffed clinics and designated foreigners' clinics in local hospitals with English-speaking personnel. For more serious and complicated issues, patients often return to their home countries or seek treatment in Hong Kong. Similarly, all the medication you might need – over-the-counter and prescription – should be brought with you, as not all medication can be found in Shanghai under the same brand names as back home.

### Hospitals and clinics

**Shanghai Huashan Hospital Foreigner's Ward**; 19/F, 12 Wulumuqi Middle Road; tel: 6248 9999 ext 1900. A mid-sized general hospital which offers most specialities except obstetrics and gynaecology, and paediatrics.

**Pudong Children's Medical Centre**; 1678 Dongfang Road, Pudong; tel: 5873 2020. A large, modern teaching hospital built as a Sino-US joint venture.

**Ruijin Hospital**; 197 Ruijin No. 2 Road; tel: 6437 0045, ext 8101 (outpatients and emergencies only); 6324 0090 ext 2101 (24-hour house calls). Large teaching hospital. The foreigners' clinic is located in Guang Ci Hospital, in the grounds.

**Parkway Health, Shanghai Centre Clinic**; Suite 203, West Retail Plaza, Shanghai Centre, 1376 Nanjing Road West; tel: 6445 5999; www.parkway health.cn. Reputable clinic with overseas-trained and English-speaking doctors and staff. Operates clinics throughout the city. For 24-hour assistance, call 6445 5999.

### Pharmacies

Parkway Health centres will fill prescriptions (see above).

**Shanghai No. 1 Dispensary**; 616 Nanjing Road East; tel: 6322 4567; daily 9am–10pm.

**Watsons**; 789 Huaihai Middle Road; tel: 6474 4775; daily 9am–10pm. Branches all over the city.

## HOLIDAYS

**New Year's Day:** 1 Jan

**Spring Festival:** Jan/Feb*
**Qing Ming:** Apr*
**Labour Day:** 1 May
**Dragon Boat Festival:** June*
**Mid-Autumn Festival:** Sept/Oct*
**National Day:** 1 Oct

Note that Spring Festival (or Chinese New Year) and National Day are often week-long holidays. Schools and government offices are open the weekend before or after the one-week holiday. Spring Festival and National Day holidays signal a huge migration of travellers across China, and trains, airlines and hotels are booked out well in advance. (*Denotes holidays determined by the lunar calendar, with slightly different dates each year.)

## HOURS

Offices open Monday to Friday 9am–6pm. Government offices are open 9am–5pm during weekdays with a 1–2-hour lunch break. Banks may stay open until 6 or 7pm; some currency exchange desks are open around the clock, and ATMs are everywhere.

Most large malls and department stores open from 10am–10pm, seven days a week. Smaller shops may have shorter hours. Keep in mind that most businesses are closed during Chinese New Year and other national holidays.

## I

## ID

Visitors should carry with them a form of photo identification, such as passport, or a photocopy of it at all times.

### INTERNET

Most business hotels either have in-room Wi-Fi or broadband access. There are wireless cafés all over the city as well.

## L

### LANGUAGE

Shanghai's official language is Mandarin (Putonghua). Local residents also converse in the Shanghainese dialect. English is increasingly understood by the younger generations in central areas (though not by taxi drivers so always have your destinations written in characters). Street names, public transport and utilities signage is written in Chinese and Pinyin (phonetic) or English translation, as are many restaurant menus.

## M

### MAPS

Free tourist maps of Shanghai in English and Chinese are available at the airport and from most hotels. The maps sold at the bookshops are usually in Chinese. Recommended is the *Insight Fleximap Shanghai*, laminated for durability.

### MEDIA

#### Newspapers and Magazines

*Shanghai Daily* (www.shanghaidaily. com) and Beijing-based *China Daily* (www.chinadaily.com) are both pub-lished in English. Foreign newspapers and publications are available from the city's four- and five-star hotels. One of the best sources is The Portman Ritz-Carlton Shanghai, which carries the *South China Morning Post*, *International Herald Tribune*, *Asian Wall Street Journal* and magazines like *Economist*, *Time* and *Newsweek*.

Shanghai is awash with free English-language publications of varying quality, most with useful listings of restaurants, bars and entertainment spots. Among the best are *Time Out* (www.timeoutshanghai. com) and *City Weekend* (www.city weekend.com.cn).

#### Radio

BBC World Service is accessible on radio. English-language programming is on FM 101.7 and FM 103.7.

#### Television

Shanghai has two English language channels. News and cultural programmes are broadcast on China Central Television (CCTV) Channel 9, while ICS is a locally produced channel with slightly more entertaining programming, including foreign movies. Most hotels offer a range of international cable and satellite channels.

### MONEY

The Chinese yuan (CNY) is also known as renminbi (RMB). One yuan or renminbi (colloquially called *kuai*) is divided into 10 jiao (colloquially known as *mao*); one jiao is divided into 10 fen. RMB bills are issued by the Bank of China in the following denominations: one, five, 10, 50 and 100. Coins come in denominations of one *kuai*, and 50, 10 and five fen.

### Changing money

Exchange rates are uniform regardless of whether you change money at a bank or hotel. Major currencies can be changed at hotels (but you must be a registered guest) as well as at banks. The same applies for traveller's cheques. Slightly better exchange rates are offered for traveller's cheques as opposed to cash.

### Credit cards and ATMs

International credit cards and bankcards (Cirrus, Plus, Visa, MasterCard, American Express) can be used to withdraw local currency from ATMs, which are found throughout the city. International credit cards are now accepted at major hotels and most restaurants – although many Chinese restaurants and small hotels only take cash or domestic credit cards. Cash is also king in the markets and small local shops.

## P

### POST

Every neighbourhood in Shanghai city has a post office, recognisable by its dark green and yellow signage. Post offices in the busiest areas, ie Sichuan Road, Huaihai Middle Road, Nanjing Road and Xujiahui, are open 14 hours, while the Huangpu district post office is open 24 hours. In addition to mailing and selling stamps,

post offices also deliver local courier packages. Most large hotels will post letters to international destinations for you.

## T

### TELEPHONES

The country code for China is 86; the city code for Shanghai is 021. When calling Shanghai from overseas, drop the prefix zero. When making a domestic call from one province to another in China, dial the city code first (including the prefix zero). Local calls within Shanghai do not require the city code. To make an international direct dial call from Shanghai, dial the international access code 00, followed by the country code, the area code and the local telephone number.
Local directory assistance: 114
International operator: 116

Most public telephones in China use prepaid phone cards, which can be used for local, long- distance and international (IDD) calls. Prepaid phone cards are available in amounts of RMB20, 30, 50 and 100.

### Mobile (cell) phones

To avoid roaming charges, get a prepaid SIM card with a local number and fixed number of minutes. Many phone providers, hotels, convenience stores and self-serve kiosks at airports sell them in denominations of RMB100. Calls are charged by the minute. The main service providers are Shanghai Telecom, Shanghai Mobile and China Unicom.

## TIME

Shanghai (and all of China) is on Beijing time, which is 8 hours ahead of Greenwich Mean Time (GMT).

## TIPPING

Locals do not generally tip and it is not usually expected. For taxis and many restaurants, you needn't tip, but in international restaurants it is becoming accepted. RMB 10 per day is reasonable for a tour guide. Hotels and some high-end restaurants add a 15 per cent service charge to bills automatically.

## TOURIST INFORMATION

A tourist hotline (tel: 962 020) operates daily from 10am to 9pm. Information can be patchy depending on who you get on the line. Be sure to ask for an operator who speaks English. **The Shanghai Tourist Information and Service Centre** (http://lyw.sh.gov.cn/en) operates branches in each of Shanghai's districts, including one on the ground level of the arrival hall of Pudong International Airport, though these are geared towards Chinese-speaking travellers. Hotel concierges in five-star hotels and local tourist magazines and websites are generally the best source of current information. *City Weekend* (www.cityweekend.com.cn) has a useful text messaging service that sends addresses in Chinese to your mobile phone.

## TRANSPORT

Shanghai has an efficient, easy-to-use and well-priced transport system.

## Arriving by Air

Shanghai has two airports (www.shairport.com): **Pudong International Airport** (30km east of the city centre – code PVG) is mainly for international flights. **Hongqiao Airport** (15km west of the city – SHA) is for domestic flights and some Hong Kong, Taiwan and South Korean routes. Getting from both airports to the city is straightforward. **From Pudong**: official taxis into the city cost RMB80–150, depending on your destination. The MagLev train (one way RMB40 with same-day air ticket, return RMB80) links with Longyang Road metro station (metro line 2) in Pudong – from here, catch a metro or taxi to your onward destination. Eight air-conditioned airport bus routes transport passengers around the city (RMB18–30, route details are posted in the arrivals hall). **From Hongqiao**: The Hongqiao Transport Hub connects Terminal 2 with metro lines 2 and 10, Hongqiao Railway Station and the long-distance bus station. Terminal 1 connects with metro line 10 only. Taxis are easily available and cost between RMB20–100 to downtown, depending on destination.

## Getting around

**Bus:** Shanghai's bus system can be confusing for visitors and bus routes are in Chinese characters. Taxis, which are very cheap, or the metro are better options. Uber services are a popular option for foreigners in Shanghai.
**Metro:** Shanghai has the longest

metro system in the world, and it's still growing. Shanghai currently has 14 metro lines (with several more under construction) running all across the city from around 6am to midnight. Everything is signposted in English and Chinese, and on-train stop announcements are multi-lingual. Metro line 2 connects Pudong International Airport in the east with Hongqiao Airport in the far west but it takes ages – a better bet is to take the MagLev then switch to Line 2.

**Taxis:** Taxis are easy to hail on the street, outside rush hours – Dazhong (96822) and Jingjiang (96961) are reputable companies. Fares are cheap and always metered, and receipts are given if requested. Flag fall is RMB14 (RMB165 after 11pm) for the first 3km, and RMB2.4 per km thereafter. Tipping is not expected.

### V

## VISAS

Most visitors to China require a pre-arranged visa. There are several ways of procuring one. The easiest way is to use the services of a travel agent. There will be a commission charge on top of the visa-processing fee paid to the visa office of the Chinese embassy or consulate. Individual travellers may also apply for a visa directly with the Chinese embassy or consulate in their home country. Two passport-size photos, the completed application form and the fee are required. It takes about 7–10 working days to process your China visa, so make sure you apply for one well before your intended departure.

Residents of 51 countries, including the UK, US, Canada and Australia, can obtain a free 72-hour visa to visit Shanghai while in transit to other destinations. Note that this only applies when you are visiting one Chinese city – you cannot, for instance, enjoy a 72 hour stay in Shanghai and then fly to Beijing.

###  W

## WEBSITES

The following websites provide a variety of information on travel-related subjects on Shanghai.

**General information**
www.china.org.cn

**China Foreign Ministry**
www.fmprc.gov.cn/eng

**Shanghai government**
www.shanghai.gov.cn
www.investment.gov.cn

**Health matters**
www.worldlink-shanghai.com

**Banks in Shanghai**
www.sbacn.org

**Airport information**
www.shanghaiairport.com

**Government travel services**
www.cits.net
www.ctsho.com
www.cnto.org
www.cnta.gov.cn

**Entertainment and events**
www.cityweekend.com.cn
www.timeoutshanghai.com
www.smartshanghai.com

**Hotel bookings**
www.ctrip.com
www.elong.com

# INDEX

Experience Shanghai
Editor: Sarah Clark
Author: Amy Fabris-Shi
Head of Production: Rebeka Davies
Picture Editor: Tom Smyth
Cartography: original cartography Apa
Cartography Department, updated by Carte
Photography: Alamy 32, 37, 90, 91, 101,
105, 108, 120, 127, 139, 144, 146, 153,
155; Alfred Dunhill 95; Chee Hong 104;
Chris Cypert/Ritz-Carlton 116; Corbis
143; David Shen Kai/Apa Publications 18,
56, 73, 76/77, 80, 81, 93, 103, 109, 124,
125, 151, 152, 162; Faimouioui 157; Farine
79, 96; Getty Images 4/5, 6, 8T, 10, 11B,
19B, 21, 24, 28, 36, 41, 45, 46, 51, 55, 64,
82, 86, 98, 99, 102, 110, 115, 117, 126,
132, 134, 140, 145, 150, 158, 159, 160,
163; Hilton Worldwide 12/13, 31; Hyatt
Corporation 11T; Imaginechina 17, 42, 44,
53, 84, 94, 106, 107, 119, 133, 135, 136,
154, 156; Imaginechina/REX/Shutterstock
61; Insiders Experience 97; iStock 71, 85,
122, 128; Jason Atherton 59; Jumeirah
International LLC 123; Leonardo 8B, 30,
74; Lost Heaven 62; M on the Bund 38; Mr
& Mrs Bund 9, 34; Peninsula Hotels 35;
Public domain 40; Robert Harding 142;
Ryan Pyle/Apa Publications 14, 15, 19T,
43, 50, 52, 57, 58, 69, 70, 75, 78, 83, 92;
Shutterstock 1, 16, 33, 60, 72, 118, 121,
141, 161; SuperStock 63; The Bund Tea
Company 39
Cover: iStock

**Distribution**
**UK, Ireland and Europe**
Apa Publications (UK) Ltd
sales@insightguides.com
**United States and Canada**
Ingram Publisher Services
ips@ingramcontent.com
**Australia and New Zealand**
Woodslane
info@woodslane.com.au

**Southeast Asia**
Apa Publications (SN) Pte
singaporeoffice@insightguides.com
**Hong Kong, Taiwan and China**
Apa Publications (HK) Ltd
hongkongoffice@insightguides.com
**Worldwide**
Apa Publications (UK) Ltd
sales@insightguides.com

**Special Sales, Content Licensing
and CoPublishing**
Insight Guides can be purchased in bulk
quantities at discounted prices. We can
create special editions, personalised
jackets and corporate imprints tailored to
your needs.
sales@insightguides.com
www.insightguides.biz

First Edition 2016

**Contact us**
Every effort has been made to provide
accurate information in this publication,
but changes are inevitable. The publisher
cannot be responsible for any resulting
loss, inconvenience or injury. We would
appreciate it if readers would call our
attention to any errors or outdated
information. We also welcome your
suggestions; please contact us at:
hello@insightguides.com
www.insightguides.com

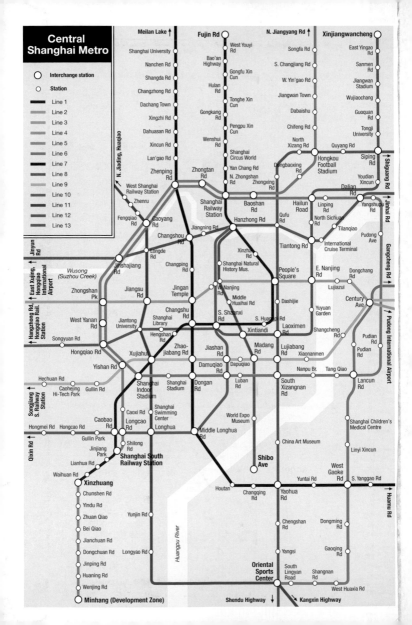

**INSIGHT** ⊙ **GUIDES**
TRAVEL MADE EASY. ASK LOCAL EXPERTS.

# UNIQUE HOLIDAYS, CHOSEN BY YOU
## Dream it. Find it. Book it.

**COLLECT YOUR VOUCHER**
insightguides.com/books2016
code: BOOKS2016